Centers of Excellence

Centers of Excellence

Niche Methods to Improve Higher Education in the 21st Century

Edited by Darrel W. Staat

ROWMAN & LITTLEFIELD
Lanham • Boulder • New York • London

Published by Rowman & Littlefield
An imprint of The Rowman & Littlefield Publishing Group, Inc.
4501 Forbes Boulevard, Suite 200, Lanham, Maryland 20706
www.rowman.com

86-90 Paul Street, London EC2A 4NE, United Kingdom

Copyright © 2022 by Darrel W. Staat

All rights reserved. No part of this book may be reproduced in any form or by any electronic or mechanical means, including information storage and retrieval systems, without written permission from the publisher, except by a reviewer who may quote passages in a review.

British Library Cataloguing in Publication Information Available

Library of Congress Cataloging-in-Publication Data

Names: Staat, Darrel W., 1941- editor.
Title: Centers of excellence : niche methods to improve higher education in 21st century / Edited by Darrel W. Staat.
Description: Lanham : Rowman & Littlefield, [2022] | Summary: "Centers of Excellence helps higher education institutions understand the value of Centers of Excellence and the methods required to initiate one. This book also informs students how these centers can provide assistance to their future employment as well as explains how higher education can work with the business community in their employee search"—Provided by publisher.
Identifiers: LCCN 2022013300 (print) | LCCN 2022013301 (ebook) | ISBN 9781475866575 (cloth) | ISBN 9781475866582 (paperback) | ISBN 9781475866599 (epub)
Subjects: LCSH: Education, Higher—Aims and objectives. | Universities and colleges—Planning. | Continuing education centers—Planning. | Business and education. | School-to-work transition.
Classification: LCC LB2322.2 .C42 2022 (print) | LCC LB2322.2 (ebook) | DDC 378.1—dc23/eng/20220503
LC record available at https://lccn.loc.gov/2022013300
LC ebook record available at https://lccn.loc.gov/2022013301

Contents

Preface	vii
Acknowledgments	ix
Introduction	xi
Chapter 1: Center of Excellence for Community College Teaching *Kara McLain Finch*	1
Chapter 2: Center of Excellence for Energy Regulation and Policy Analysis *Cory Glasser*	13
Chapter 3: Center of Excellence for Cybersecurity *Pamela Shortt*	25
Chapter 4: Center of Excellence for Biotechnology *Diana Cavender Dymek*	37
Chapter 5: Center of Excellence for Business *Roy E. Allen*	49
Chapter 6: Center of Excellence for Agriculture and Water *Von Locklear*	59
Chapter 7: Center of Excellence for International Studies *Timothy Gwillim*	71
Chapter 8: Center of Excellence for Learning Sciences *Shawn Guy*	83

Chapter 9: Center of Excellence for Manufacturing Innovation 93
　　Mark T. Rooze

Chapter 10: Center of Excellence for Pharmacy 105
　　Candice Geiger

Chapter 11: Center of Excellence for University Teaching 115
　　Amber Lennon-Harmon

Chapter 12: Center of Excellence for Manufacturing and
　　Technology 127
　　Lauren Holland

Epilogue 137

About the Editor 139

About the Contributors 141

Preface

In higher education in the twenty-first century, a number of Centers of Excellence (COE) are developing in both community colleges and universities. As of the writing of this book, there does not seem to be a national association of Centers of Excellence in Higher Education. Rather, the COEs that are developing in various states are mostly contained within a discipline or a medical field. Further, there are no agreed upon definitions of what a COE is or should be. The area is wide open to interpretation at the community college and university level.

The situation that COEs exist with no tangible connection to each other or that follow no set of guidelines as to what a COE should be allows them to develop in different ways. It also led to the idea for this book. Since there was no way to sensibly cover all the centers that exist in higher education institutions in the United States, it was decided to research twelve Centers of Excellence, some in community colleges and others in universities. Consequently, a set of twelve graduate students researched a dozen Centers in higher education, The findings give the reader an idea of what exists and some insight into the quality of instruction, the faculty involved, and the value to students.

The Centers of Excellence covered are found in a variety of states:

The findings of the research were eye-opening. Not only did the Centers follow no set guidelines, they also varied in development. All are successful in fulfilling their vision and mission to one degree or another. The research gives the reader an idea of what it takes to initiate

Table 0.1.

State	Higher Education Institution	Center of Excellence
Kentucky	Blue Grass Community College	Cyber Defense
Maryland	Howard Community College	Teaching
Michigan	Saginaw Valley State	Business
Nebraska	Northeast Community College	Agriculture & Water
North Carolina	Forsyth Community College	Cyber Defense
North Carolina	University of North Carolina Wilmington	Teaching
Pennsylvania	Community College of Philadelphia	International Studies
South Carolina	Greenville Technical College	Advanced Manufacturing
South Carolina	Southeastern Institute of Manufacturing and Technology	Manufacturing and Technology
South Carolina	University of South Carolina	Pharmacy
Tennessee	Tennessee State University	Learning Sciences
Wyoming	University of Wyoming	Energy Regulation and Policy Analysis

a center, keep it operational with high quality, and retain its viable over an extended period of time for the institution and its students.

While on one hand, that fact that there are no guidelines or regulations for a Center of Excellence gives those interested in developing one free rein. On the other hand, creating a successful center over the long term often proves to be an arduous task. Those who are successful usually have a leader with a mission and vision that is valuable to the institution and the students it serves. Funding comes from a variety of sources including state General Assemblies, grants, investors, and institutions themselves. It takes determination coupled with excellent leadership skills to create and keep a center viable over the long run.

Acknowledgments

I would like to express my sincere thanks to the graduate students of Cohort 8 in the Higher Education Executive Leadership Program at Wingate University. Their individual research and diligent work in completing a graduate course entitled *Higher Education in the Twenty-First Century* resulted in the development and writing of the chapters in this book. I greatly appreciate the interest, enthusiasm, and effort of the students who made this book possible.

I would also thank Dr. Charlesa Hann, dean of graduate programs in the Thayer School of Education at Wingate University. Her encouragement and support are greatly appreciated.

As always, I thank my wonderful wife Beverly who understands and supports the time and effort that developing a book such as this entails.

Introduction

The twenty-first century has seen a number of institutions of higher education develop and implement Centers of Excellence (COE) in a variety of disciplines. COEs were sometimes provided with funding in excess of what would produce a normal, successful disciplinary program. That type of funding allowed for obtaining highly specialized faculty, state of the art equipment, and when required, specifically designed facilities. The sources of funding for COEs include federal grants, special allocations from the state General Assemblies, fund-raising projects, donations from supporting businesses, and individuals who have significant interest in the development of a center.

Whatever the source of funding, COEs exist in community colleges and universities to provide students with education and training at the highest level, support the business community with superb candidates for employment, and increase the status of the community college or university involved. Without any doubt, Centers of Excellence have found a niche in higher education in the twenty-first century and have the potential to become leaders in the discipline they are part of nationally and, in some cases, globally.

This book identifies twelve centers, seven in community colleges and five in universities which help to define what a COE is, what it takes to operate, who it attracts in terms of students and what it provides to the organizations that hire the graduates. Centers of Excellence have the potential to become leaders in education today and as the century progresses. COEs are not a flash in the pan but solid, academic attempts keep higher education at the bleeding edge of what exists today and what may arrive in the near future.

Potential students may find the book interesting in terms of which institutions are supporting the COEs. Faculty interested in working in a center or initiating one may find this book an excellent starting point for their future careers, and employers may find specific centers much to their liking when searching for graduates to hire. Finally, a successful Center of Excellence can raise the credibility of the institution considerably making recruitment easier, causing retention to become almost a certainty, and producing graduates who demonstrate the value of the high-quality instruction and experience that the centers produce.

Chapter 1

Center of Excellence for Community College Teaching

Kara McLain Finch

Howard Community College (HCC), located in Columbia, Maryland, is just 35 minutes south of Baltimore and 50 minutes north of Washington, D.C. HCC was founded in 1966 and is one of 16 community colleges located in Maryland. The governor of Maryland appoints seven citizens to serve six-year terms as the college's legal governing body and Dr. Kathleen B. Hetherington is the current President of the institution. The institution's operating budget for fiscal year 2020 was $123,159,664 (Office of the President, 2021).

PROGRAM OFFERINGS

Howard Community College offers two-year degree and certificate programs. Students can attend classes in multiple locations with flexible scheduling. Online, hybrid, and accelerated learning formats are offered to meet the varying needs of the students served.

Howard Community College is accredited by the Middle States Commission on Higher Education (MSCHE) and authorized by the Maryland Higher Education Commission (MHEC) to offer programs and award certificates of proficiency and associates in arts degrees.

An extensive reaccreditation process is completed every eight years (Howard Community College about us Policies and Procedures, 2021).

Additional programs offered at HCC are accredited by their respective accrediting bodies. These programs include Nursing and Allied Health, Arts and Humanities, and Business and Computers. The institution also holds membership with the American Association of Community Colleges, the National Association of College and University Business Officers, the National Association of Community College Trustees, the National Accrediting Commission, National League for Nursing, and Maryland Association of Community Colleges (Howard Community College at a Glance, 2021).

MALCOLM BALDRIGE AWARD

Howard Community College received the Malcolm Baldrige National Quality Award in 2019, the nation's only presidential-level honor for performance excellence in organizations. The mission, vision, and values of Howard Community College provide guidance on how the institution should operate and their priorities. The institution's mission is providing pathways to success, while the institution's vision is to be a place to discover greatness in oneself and others.

Howard Community College has eight specific values of focus, innovation, nurturing, service and sustainability, partnerships, integrity, respect, excellence, and diversity, equity, and inclusion (Howard Community College about us Baldridge, 2019).

The institution believes that to be an excellent organization, the mission, vision, and values must be understood. External and internal communities collaborate on the development of the institution's strategic plan every five years. The 2021–2025 strategic goals are student success, completion, and lifelong learning, organizational excellence, and building and sustaining partnerships (Howard Community College about us Mission, 2021).

DESCRIPTION AND PURPOSE OF THE CENTER

The Center for Teaching Excellence (CTE) at Howard Community College supports faculty with resources to enhance teaching and learning. Faculty can receive comprehensive instructional design services that integrate coaching, research-based best practices in teaching, and consulting (A. Martin, personal communication, May 11, 2021). Assistance with course, lesson, assignment, and assessment design is also provided to faculty. This service is provided to assist faculty with aligning their design with learning objectives and outcomes.

Assistance with classroom technologies and teaching methods to increase flexibility and in-classroom support is another service provided by the center. Faculty can also receive support for instructional innovations and have access to lab space allowing them to explore new technology (Faculty and Staff Resources, 2021).

The CTE also encourages faculty collaboration and offers opportunities for faculty to offer workshops on best practices in teaching and learning. Support is also provided to faculty when working on projects, initiatives, and presentations. Additional support with capturing faculty lectures and media creation is provided, and faculty at HCC always have access to the CTE online resources.

Operation of the Center

In 2018, the Faculty Development Department was re-established as the Howard Community College Center for Teaching Excellence. Amy Chase Martin, Director of Faculty Development and Instructional Media provides the daily oversight of the CTE. Martin supervises four employees who assist with the daily operations of the center. The services provided by the CTE are confidential. Faculty are encouraged to come to the Center with any questions and the support team will connect them to the right answers. The CTE provides judgment free support and assistance (A. Martin, personal communication, May 11, 2021).

The Center for Teaching Excellence at HCC provides comprehensive instructional design support with consultation and instructional materials review. The CTE staff also provide in-class coaching and support which includes assistance with technology and classroom teaching methods. The CTE has a comprehensive library of teaching resources available to all faculty. Faculty lab space is provided to encourage exploration of new technology.

Faculty can also use the lab space to meet with an instructional designer for support. The CTE provides support to faculty in reviewing course evaluations and makes suggestions for improvement in course design. Faculty can use the CTE to record material for their courses, and access editing software to create instructional media (Faculty and Staff Resources, 2021).

Purpose of the Center

The primary focus of the Center for Teaching Excellence is face-to-face instruction. *Quality Matters* is the framework used to ensure quality of all courses at HCC. Prior to the COVID-19 pandemic, only 30% of courses at Howard Community College were taught online. Currently, there are no fully online curriculum programs at the institution When the COVID-19 pandemic required shutdown of the institution, classes were cancelled for two days to provide professional development and assistance to faculty.

Due to most faculty providing face-to-face instruction, much work had to be done to move all instruction to Canvas, the institution's learning management system. The CTE partnered with e-Learning to train over 425 fulltime and adjunct faculty on how to conduct remote instruction. This was achieved in those two full days of workshops. The COVID-19 pandemic prompted the development of the Keep Teaching and Keep Learning areas of the CTE website. Faculty used these resources to help them prepare and continue to provide rigorous and quality instruction.

Resources include guides to teaching remotely, including how to use Zoom to schedule meetings with students and provide instruction. A tool, *10 Steps to Keep Teaching,* was developed that provides faculty with information and directions on how to download necessary technology, facilitate assessments with effective monitoring, and provide appropriate feedback and post grades. All faculty at HCC have access to these resources; however, some resources must be accessed by logging in with faculty credentials (Faculty and Staff Resources, 2021).

Services of the Center

The services and support provided by the Center for Teaching Excellence are available for use by all full-time faculty and adjunct faculty members. Newsletters are regularly developed with new techniques and skills that faculty can use in their classrooms. These newsletters also provide information related to upcoming professional development opportunities. The current and past newsletters can be accessed from the professional development link of the CTE.

Staff and Faculty

The staff at the Center for Teaching Excellence are also trained to address behavioral issues in classrooms. Faculty with behavioral concerns in the classroom can request an observation from the CTE staff after which recommendations can be provided to assist faculty in addressing behavior issues in the classroom. The CTE at HCC also provides an excellent resource for faculty to better prepare for their new courses.

Often, faculty will be assigned new classrooms each semester, and adjunct faculty rarely see the campus before they embark on the first session of a course. The CTE developed an area on their website that allows faculty to view their classroom prior to the first day of class. Faculty can just simply click on the classroom they have been assigned on the website and take a virtual tour of the classroom. This not only helps faculty with familiarity of their classroom, but also allows them to address any concerns related to classroom setup and technology (A. Martin, personal communication, May 11, 2021).

The Center for Teaching Excellence provides access to current educational technologies that faculty can use to enhance their classes and meet learning objectives. A tech finder tool helps faculty find recommended tools for a variety of needs.

Faculty can simply click on the link related to what they wish to do, such as communication with students, discussion facilitation, presentation of instructional material, recording videos, developing quizzes to evaluate students, use of classroom equipment, and more. Each area provides a list of links to tools that can be used to effectively meet one of the needs previously mentioned (Howard Community College News Events, 2021).

Many of the workshops offered by the Center for Teaching Excellence are recorded and available for access later along with the power point presentations. The Faculty Development Library was created to share books that advocate teaching excellence. Each book shared is also available for faculty to check out from the institution's library. Faculty and staff are encouraged to share resources that can be added to the development library (CTE Faculty Workshop Resources, 2021).

STUDENTS

The student to faculty ratio at Howard Community College is nineteen to one. The institution employs 2,577 faculty and staff members. In 2021, there were 14,314 credit students and 12,313 noncredit continuing education students. An additional 8,732 noncredit students are enrolled in workforce development training classes at HCC. 28% of credit students attend HCC full-time, while 72% attend part-time. The average age of students at the institution is 25 years old and 106 different countries are represented by the student body.

The ethnicity of credit students is 32% White, 29% African American, 15% Asian, 12% Hispanic, and 14% other. 75% of the students attending HCC are from Howard County, 23% are from another county in Maryland, and 1% of students attending are from out-of-state. Returning students account for 70% of the institution's student population, 4% are first-time students, 5% are transfer students, and 19% are concurrently enrolled (Spotlight Howard Community College, 2021).

EDUCATIONAL PROGRAM OBJECTIVES

The educational program at Howard Community College has three major objectives. The program focuses on helping students grow in their ability to live effectively in society, providing students with access to enriched and expanded lives, and providing a foundation for students to transfer to other institutions of higher education. Full-time faculty are expected to perform at a commendable level.

TEACHING LOADS

Faculty are evaluated based on their performance in general teaching responsibilities, college responsibilities, divisional responsibilities, instructional improvement activities, professional development, and learning outcomes assessments. Faculty are expected to demonstrate quality teaching and are required to teach 14–16 credits per semester. All faculty at HCC are expected to participate in activities that improve their teaching and student learning.

All new faculty are required to complete new faculty orientation prior to teaching with the institution. Professional development activities designed to update knowledge and skills that support teaching excellence are required. Full-time faculty must participate in 10 hours of onsite professional development each year, while adjunct faculty are expected to attend requirement meetings, professional development activities, and trainings.

Each year, the CTE plans and develops the Adjunct Institute, a one-day professional development conference for adjunct faculty. This program is not required but is free for all adjunct faculty at HCC. Over 125 adjunct faculty attended the last Adjunct Institute (A. Martin, personal communication, May 11, 2021). Faculty and staff at HCC are provided resources to assist students with tutoring and learning assistance, interpreter services, counseling services, and working with students with disabilities (Support Services, 2021).

OUTCOMES OF THE CENTER

The Center for Teaching Excellence at HCC encourages faculty and staff to share best practices at professional development meetings, conferences, and professional organizations. The sharing of best practices enriches the completion at the institution. The IDEA Survey, Howard Community College's course evaluation system, is completed by students during the last three weeks of the semester. Completing this survey gives students the opportunity to provide feedback on the courses completed and the instructors. These evaluations are completed online, and the feedback is anonymous.

Survey Monitoring

Survey data is provided to each faculty member for use in course reviews and developing improvements. The CTE not only monitors the course evaluations, but also provides workshops to help faculty understand how to interpret the results of their IDEA surveys. Faculty are also given the opportunity to participate in one-on-one consultations with a member of the professional development team (CTE Faculty IDEA Evaluations, 2021). Faculty have access to the Learning Objectives Selection Form.

This tool assists faculty in identifying the relevance of their course objectives. Faculty can prioritize what they want students to learn by identifying important objectives, essential objectives, and minor objectives. The IDEA surveys can be used to determine areas for improvement and develop professional development activities for faculty.

The Center for Teaching Excellence has seen an increase in participation in the Adjunct Institute with just 32 participants in the first year to 125 participants in the third year. The training provided to adjunct faculty through the CTE on classroom technology prior to the beginning of each major semester has reduced calls received by audio visual services by two-third in the first week of classes.

Center Growth

The CTE has also seen a 12% growth each year in consultations with faculty receiving coaching on instructional design, teaching techniques and technology use. Annually, the CTE offers 60 workshops available to faculty and staff. With the COVID-19 pandemic and the move to remote learning, 127 virtual sessions were offered. The use of the institution's lecture capture and video streaming platform, managed by the CTE, had 350% growth in usage with the move to remote instruction (A. Martin, personal communication, May 11, 2021).

STRENGTHS AND IMPROVEMENTS NEEDED

One of the strengths of the Center for Teaching Excellence is its leadership and team. Each team member has experience and training in their respective roles. Martin has years of experience as a corporate trainer and instructional designer. Her experience and education have allowed her to effectively support the faculty at Howard Community College with excellent training and services to help them meet the needs of their students.

Another strength of the Center for Teaching Excellence is its commitment to excellence and responsiveness. The team evaluates each gap in instruction and service delivery and tries to continually adjust and respond to the needs of faculty and students. The team also works hours to meet the needs of the population served. Most often, adjuncts are not available during normal working hours and faculty are not always building lessons during the week as they are teaching classes. The CTE team tries to respond in a timely manner, regardless of the time a request is received.

While there are multiple strengths identified, there are also areas that need improvement at the Center for Teaching Excellence. One of these needed improvements is additional staff. The CTE recently added one additional full-time staff member, which raised their number to four. The support services provided to the number of faculty and students often requires a lot of time and resources. The CTE would benefit from additional staff to help support their mission (A. Martin, personal communication, May 11, 2021).

VALUE OF THE CENTER FOR STUDENTS

In addition to the resources provided to faculty by the Center for Teaching Excellence, students are also provided with online resources to help them successfully learn remotely. All students are required to use Canvas (an online format), whether they are enrolled in online, hybrid, or face-to-face courses. Students use the learning management system to communicate with instructors and other students, complete required tasks, and to review course content such as the course syllabus.

The resources provided by the CTE support student use tools should their course be quickly and unexpectedly moved online. Students are also provided with a quick guide for help and support services for assistance with Canvas, login help, technology help, and public safety. Students can also access a variety of resources and extra help on the Center for Teaching Excellence webpage.

These resources include information on accessibility, assistance with assignments, assistance with writing, and tutoring. Students can also access information on additional resources such as counseling, admissions, career services, disability services, financial aid, food pantry assistance, and more (CTE Faculty Workshop Resources, 2021).

VALUE OF THE CENTER TO SERVICE AREA OF THE INSTITUTION

Training and Development Solutions by Howard Community College provides workforce training to local business and industry. While this is not a part of the Center for Teaching Excellence, many business and industry partners have requested more online training solutions due to the COVID-19 pandemic. The resources developed to assist faculty with online instruction is also available to those working with business and industry in the community.

Instruction is provided directly, when invited, to the instructors providing training to the workforce. Workshops on various technology tools, training on the design of rubrics, and training on first day strategies have been provided. The CTE has also provided some consultations on the design of instruction.

The Maryland Innovation Center (MIC) is four miles from the Howard Community College campus. The MIC provides guidance, resources, and support to help business owner grow and manage their business. The Howard Community College Training and Development solutions serves as the education and training division of the MIC. These partnerships also increase career opportunities to graduating students at HCC. Faculty and staff work closely with local business and industry to ensure that students are being effectively prepared for the workforce (Spotlight Howard Community College, 2021).

CONCLUSION

The CTE is working with faculty to infuse soft skills development into their curriculum. Doing so will improve career outcomes for students and move students from enrollment at HCC to employment. Those mastering soft skills can significantly contribute to the success of the workplace. Some examples of how this may be provided in the future is through seminars, orientation, webinars, incorporating them into the general studies curriculum, or adding them to all core curriculum programs throughout the institution.

The CTE plans to start triangulating workshop attendance, course evaluation, and student performance and retention data beginning Spring 2022. The CTE at Howard Community College remains focused on providing quality training and support in instructional design, technology use, and teaching techniques for all faculty at the institution.

REFERENCES

CTE Faculty Idea Evaluations. (May 10, 2021). Retrieved from https://ctefaculty.com/idea-evaluations.html

CTE Faculty Workshop Resources. (May 10, 2021). Retrieved from https://ctefaculty.com/workshop-resources.html

Faculty and Staff Resources. (May 10, 2021). Retrieved from https://faculty-and-staff-support/resources/facultyandstaffresources/faculty-resources/instructional-media/learning-technologies.html

Howard Community College about us Baldrige. Retrieved from https://www.howardcc.edu/about-us/baldridge/documents/2019%20Balddrige%20Application.pdf

Howard Community College about us Mission. (May 20, 2021). Retrieved from https://howardcc.edu/about-us/mission-and-strategic-plan/commission-on-future/documents/January_2018Final Report.pdf

Howard Community College about us Policies and Procedures. (May 20, 2021). Retrieved from https://www.howardcc.edu/about-us/policies-procedures/chapter-10/10.01.02-Faculty-Responsibilities.html

Howard Community College at a Glance. (May 10, 2021). Retrieved from https://howardcc./about-us/hcc-at-a-glance/accreditation/index.html

Howard Community College News Events. (May 15, 2021). retrieved from howardcc.edu/about-us/new-events/new/training-development-solutions-by-howard-community-college-rethinking-workforce-training-in-howard-county-and-beyond.html

Office of the President. (May 10, 2021). retrieved from https://www.howardcc.edu/about-us/leadership/office-of-the-president.html

Spotlight Howard Community College. (May 15, 2021). retrieved from https://www.aacc.nche.edu/2018/03/01/spotlight-howard-community-college.html

Support Services. (May 10, 2021). retrieved from https://howardcc.edu/services-support/academic-support/disability-support-services/faculty-staff-resources.html

Chapter 2

Center of Excellence for Energy Regulation and Policy Analysis

Cory Glasser

The University of Wyoming (UW), founded in 1886, is located in southeastern Wyoming's Laramie Mountains. UW is the state's only public four-year institution, having been established as a public land-grant university under the Morrill Act. In addition, the UW Laramie campus has expanded significantly over the years. The Laramie campus spans over 2,000 acres and houses 192 buildings totaling over seven million square feet.

With nearly 12,000 students enrolled in autumn 2020, UW prides itself on having a low student-to-faculty ratio of 15:1. Furthermore, the university offers a diverse range of academic programs, 85 undergraduate and 90 graduate degrees. In 2018, 80.3% of UW students were undergraduates and 19.7% were graduate/professional students (University of Wyoming, 2019).

Aside from the core curriculum, UW supports a considerable amount of research and economic growth for Wyoming, the region, and the country. In 2020, "UW's research enterprise generated over $97 million in grants from federal agencies, private industry, non-profit organizations, the State of Wyoming and other entities" (University of Wyoming, 2021, p. 18). UW also houses a business center, an incubator, and a number of entrepreneurial ventures.

The Wyoming Small Business Development Center, which promotes entrepreneurship throughout Wyoming, assisted in the establishment of 96 businesses in 2020, resulting in the creation and retention of 122 jobs.

Given UW's statewide prominence, general funds and budgeting are also worth noting. For the fiscal year 2020, the endowment value at the University of Wyoming Foundation was around $589 million, with more than $43 million in yearly donations. The operating budget for the fiscal year 2021 was approximately $419 million (University of Wyoming, 2021).

THE SCHOOL OF ENERGY RESOURCES

The School of Energy Resources (SER), established in 2006, is an essential part of the University of Wyoming and a source of benefit for a variety of stakeholders. SER's mission is to promote energy-driven economic growth in Wyoming through three energy-related components: academics, outreach, and research. These elements academically educate students for jobs in the state's energy industry, engage with stakeholders to aid in workforce development research, and lead technological innovation to optimize energy production while minimizing the environmental footprint (Krutka, n.d.).

SER has established more than a dozen research centers of excellence (COE) to guide its energy-driven mission; SER has eight COEs as of June 2021. These centers address a multitude of energy-related topics and encourage transdisciplinary collaboration among various UW departments and stakeholders; the current focus is on conducting extensive research on low-carbon technologies that could aid in the decarbonization of fossil fuels (K. Coddington, personal communication, June 30, 2021).

Financial Support

COEs are initially SER funded; however, financial independence is expected within a few years. Based on previous experiences, centers may depart the SER once they have achieved self-sufficiency, form new groups to address new challenges, or disband after they have achieved their objectives (School of Energy Resources, n.d.-c).

The SER is currently housed within the University of Wyoming's Energy Innovation Center (EIC), a state-of-the-art research and collaboration facility. With modern, reconfigurable laboratory spaces, "the EIC provides students, researchers, and academic professionals the opportunity to actively engage in, observe, and support advancements in sustainable energy technologies" (School of Energy Resources, n.d.-b., para. 4).

DESCRIPTION AND PURPOSE OF CERPA

The Center for Energy Regulation and Policy Analysis (CERPA) is the most recently established center of excellence at the School of Energy Resources (SER). CERPA is an "interdisciplinary organization whose purpose is to develop and integrate world-class technical, economic and regulatory policy analyses. . .and strategies to benefit the state, region and the nation" (Center for Energy Regulation and Policy Analysis, n.d.-c, (2021), para. 1).

Although CERPA was official created in 2020, a concerted effort began the summer before by combining the Center for Energy Economics and Public Policy with a broader all-encompassing interdisciplinary endeavor.

Wyoming's economy is mostly reliant on fossil fuel-related economic activity. According to the U.S. Energy Information Administration, "Wyoming produces 14 times more energy than it consumes, making it the biggest net energy supplier among the states" (Center for Energy Regulation and Policy Analysis, n.d. b, para. 1). Energy regulation and policy have a substantial impact on the state's economy as a major producer and exporter of energy. Wyoming must not only follow other states' decarbonization policies, but the federal government also has a role to play, as it owns roughly half of Wyoming's land.

The SER was established by the Wyoming legislature to conduct applied research on low-carbon technologies that could aid in the decarbonization of fossil fuels. However, over the last few years, the SER has discovered that many of these challenges are driven by legislation, policy, and regulation, not just technological issues.

CERPA was established as an interdisciplinary energy policy center to support and complement the applied technical research now underway. As a result, CERPA develops practical and sustainable energy policies and strategies to manage energy changes, particularly those affecting federal leasing (K. Coddington, personal communication, June 30, 2021).

OPERATION OF CERPA

The Center for Energy Regulation and Policy Analysis supports policymakers, decision-makers, and scientists in a variety of ways. For starters, CERPA serves as a conduit for University of Wyoming (UW) research, allowing for an all-inclusive interdisciplinary approach to energy policy and regulation. The Center draws on expertise from throughout the UW, the School of Energy Resources (SER), and other research institutes. Commonly sought-after fields include energy policy and transition, chemical and petroleum engineering, geology and geophysics, law, economics, chemistry, and so on.

Conferences

Second, through a number of channels, CERPA provides effective energy-related policy development and assessment. Conferences, symposiums, and roundtable talks are all events in which the Center actively sponsors and participates. They publish peer-reviewed papers and articles and also fund the work of others. As a co-principal investigator on multiple projects, the Center's director supports the SER's federally supported research. In addition, the Center distributes briefings to Wyoming stakeholders, including the state legislature (Center for Energy Regulation and Policy Analysis, 2020, para. 2).

Finally, CERPA supports such activities by facilitating relationships with public, private, and non-governmental institutions outside of the UW community. Wyoming is a significant energy producer and exporter in the United States, and as a result, it is subject to federal and state-level energy policies and regulations. "CERPA's work is funded by federal grants, private foundation awards, and State of Wyoming appropriations" (Center for Energy Regulation and Policy Analysis, 2020, p. 1), in reaction to shifting policies and regulations, as well as a reliance on Wyoming's energy market.

STAFFING OF CERPA

In comparison to other centers of excellence (COE), the Center for Energy Regulation and Policy Analysis (CERPA) takes a unique approach to staffing. While CERPA does a lot of work in-house, it also collaborates with members from the School of Energy Resources (SER), the University of Wyoming (UW), and other organizations. Because of its limited size and early stages of development, CERPA employs this interdisciplinary approach to support and complement the SER's applied technological research that is already ongoing.

CERPA currently employs three people: a director and two research fellows. Kipp Coddington, the director, is an expert on low-carbon technology and climate policy. He has been with the SER for more than six years and serves as co-principal investigator on several low-carbon technology projects supported by the U.S. Department of Energy. Both research fellows were hired near the end of 2020 with the help of federal grants.

One research fellow conducts public outreach and researches energy economics and policy, while the other performs substantial analysis on the state repercussions of Wyoming House Bill 200 and the Biden Administration's energy policies (School of Energy Resources, 2020b).

According to the director of CERPA, there are plans to increase the Center's staff, subject to budgetary constraints. Apart from contractual hires, it is hoped that at least one more research fellow will be hired for the fiscal year 2021–22. Similar to the other research fellows, the Center intends to seek out individuals with a solid understanding of energy policy. Although no specific academic background is required, those who have this understanding are more likely to be lawyers or economists (K. Coddington, personal communication, June 30, 2021).

OUTCOMES OF CERPA

The Center for Energy Regulation and Policy Analysis (CERPA) has accomplished a great deal in a short period of time. In general, CERPA's activity is guided and influenced by the primary goals of the School of Energy Resources (SER): research, outreach, and education. To address such goals, the Center has engaged in a variety of activities, including administration and outreach, the publication of papers and articles, and speaking engagements (School of Energy Resources, 2020a).

In terms of research, CERPA has been closely examining Wyoming House Bill 200, which examines mechanisms for deploying carbon capture and storage on certain coal-fired power plants in Wyoming. Furthermore, CERPA is now undertaking research by identifying all Wyoming energy marketplaces and examining the energy regulations in those markets. Another study conducted by CERPA looks at renewable energy systems that require relatively substantial quantities of rare earth elements and critical minerals.

Outreach

In terms of outreach, CERPA has used a variety of methods to present its findings and analyses. Over the course of two years, the Center has taken part in more than 30 webinars and other speaking engagements (School of Energy Resources, 2020a). They have a number of peer-reviewed papers and articles to their credit. Furthermore, they publish shorter, white paper versions for their target audience, Western politicians. Finally, after completing a specific study, CERPA may communicate with certain persons, such as officials from the governor's office (K. Coddington, personal communication, June 30, 2021).

Education

In terms of education, CERPA continues to work with academics, professors, and others on and off-campus. While no CERPA staff members presently teach, the director intends to teach an energy-related course in the fall of 2022. If the opportunity arises, he also encourages the research fellows to teach or give guest lectures.

STRENGTHS OF CERPA

The Center for Energy Regulation and Policy Analysis possesses a number of strengths. CERPA has established itself in just two years, largely due to the background and expertise of its team, collaboration from the School of Energy Resources, and the University of Wyoming,

Wyoming's reliance on energy, and the ever-changing state and federal policies and regulations. The Center and its personnel are the main focus of this section.

In terms of background and expertise, two of CERPA's members are non-practicing lawyers. Licensed in states other than Wyoming, neither provides legal advice to the state; however, their legal backgrounds enable them to make insightful analyses of a variety of legal, regulatory, and policy documents. The final member is an outreach professional with a background in economics and environment/natural resources.

CERPA's team is likewise technologically skilled. Although they are not formally classified as technologists, their background and experience demonstrate international level expertise in a group of technologies: carbon capture and storage (CCS) and its sister technology carbon capture, utilization, and storage (CCUS). In recent years, these technologies are widely regarded as the premier technology for decarbonizing fossil fuels.

CERPA as a whole has a thorough awareness of the present energy industry. They are not only knowledgeable about the technological components of CCS and CCUS, but they are also able to comprehend and analyze the laws, policies, and regulations that govern them. As society pushes for more stringent environmental protections—internationally, federally, or individually by state—decarbonization mandates will predominantly deploy CCS technology, an area that CERPA is deeply familiar with (K. Coddington, personal communication, June 30, 2021).

IMPROVEMENTS NEEDED OF CERPA

CERPA is still in the early phases of development. Therefore, needed improvements are mostly in the form of additional staffing; nevertheless, these are currently being addressed. The first area in need of improvement, which was resolved in July 2021, was the lack of an in-house, dedicated economist. Previously, running a complex economic model necessitated CERPA collaborating with the University of Wyoming's (UW) College of Business or seeking help from outside sources. While these collaborations were effective, schedule management and workload were two challenges that arose frequently.

Another needed improvement for CERPA is the addition of an academic-line energy policy expert. CERPA, with only administrative employees, is limited in much of the policy analysis that takes place in academics; they can interpret current writings via a legal lens, but they are missing a core analytical aspect generated from academia.

While CERPA has no plans to hire an in-house, dedicated member, they do intend to engage with the energy policy fellow that UW's HAUB School of Environment and Natural Resources is in the process of hiring. This fellow will be a classically trained academic-line energy policy expert with analytic skills to investigate the effectiveness of energy policies.

Website Needs

Aside from employing staff, CERPA's director stated a desire for a more data-rich and interactive website. CERPA is in the process of collecting and analyzing large amounts of data, much of it economic in nature. Meanwhile, the Center is also searching for a more sophisticated approach to communicate and update its intended audience. The envisioned website includes an interactive map of the United States that provides information through a Wyoming lens: energy exports to the selected state, the economic value of that export to Wyoming, and concise information about Wyoming's relevant energy policies (K. Coddington, personal communication, June 30, 2021).

ANALYSIS OF THE VALUE OF CERPA TO THE STUDENTS

CERPA is unique among other centers of excellence. Rather than focusing solely on students and the local community, it prioritizes the state of Wyoming and its residents. In the near future, the Center's director hopes to place a greater emphasis on education, such as teaching or guest lecturing. Because Wyoming is such an energy-focused state, and the University of Wyoming is the state's only public university, he believes the institution has a responsibility to ensure that graduates have a general understanding of the energy industry and policies.

ANALYSIS OF THE VALUE OF CERPA TO THE SERVICE AREA OF THE INSTITUTION

As a major producer and exporter of energy, "Wyoming's economy is influenced by a multitude of international, national, regional and state energy policies that create both opportunities and challenges for Wyoming policymakers and businesses" (Center for Energy Regulation and Policy Analysis, n.d.-a, para. 5). CERPA investigates such policies in order to provide effective energy policy development and assessment.

These findings are subsequently disseminated to various stakeholders through a variety of channels, including publications, speaking engagements, briefings, and so on. Furthermore, the Center attends a number of public and private sector informational sessions on carbon capture and storage (CCS) and other relevant issues.

CERPA VALUE NATIONALLY

CERPA is also valuable on a regional and national scale. For example, grants for applied energy projects frequently necessitate collaboration between CERPA and corporate partners. As a result, these collaborations have led to a significant amount of industry branding, such as the Energy Innovation Center's Shell 3D Visualization Center.

Furthermore, CERPA's director serves as a co-principal investigator on a number of initiatives that support the School of Energy Resources' federally funded research. Among the most recent projects, they are assisting with Wyoming's major carbon capture, utilization, and storage project in Gillette, Wyoming (Center for Energy Regulation and Policy Analysis, 2020).

FUTURE OF CERPA

The Center for Energy Regulation and Policy Analysis (CERPA) has an exciting future ahead of it. The Center's work is not only unique to Wyoming and, for the most part, the country, but it is also supported by the Wyoming legislature indirectly through the School of Energy Resources (SER). Furthermore, the type of analysis that CERPA delivers will almost certainly always be in demand. Whether it is changing federal administrations or continuing the Paris Agreement to 2050, society's drive for more stringent environmental protections will only intensify future movements (K. Coddington, personal communication, June 30, 2021).

Budgets, however, will have a significant impact on CERPA's future. Wyoming, like many other states, is facing economic challenges, forcing lawmakers to make difficult funding decisions. CERPA and the SER have worked together to broaden their funding sources, including federal grants and private foundation benefactors. They are, however, not immune to Wyoming's economic woes because they are a state entity.

The indefinite moratorium on the issuance of new federal oil and gas leases imposed by the Biden Administration, for example, has had a large and detrimental impact on Wyoming, a major producer and exporter of energy from federal lands (K. Coddington, personal communication, June 30, 2021).

CONCLUSION

CERPA is the most recently formed center of excellence at the University of Wyoming's School of Energy Resources. It complements the SER's mission of promoting energy-driven economic growth in Wyoming by addressing non-technical issues brought on by law, policy, and regulation. To that end, CERPA acts as a conduit for UW research, develops and assesses efficient energy-related policies, and supports such activities by fostering links with public, private, and non-governmental organizations outside of the UW community.

Despite being in its early stages, CERPA has established a solid foundation, largely due to the team's background and expertise, collaboration from the SER and UW, Wyoming's reliance on energy, and the ever-changing state and federal policies and regulations. CERPA as a whole is well-versed in the current energy industry. They are not only familiar with the technological components of CCS and CCUS, but they can also comprehend and analyze the laws, policies, and regulations that govern them. The type of analysis that CERPA provides will likely always be in demand since it is unique to Wyoming and, for the most part, the country.

REFERENCES

Center for Energy Regulation and Policy Analysis. (2020). Inaugural edition: Fall 2020. Retrieved from http://www.uwyo.edu/ser/research/centers-of-excellence/energy-regulation-policy/_files/cerpa-newsletter-template-v5.pdf

Center for Energy Regulation and Policy Analysis. (n.d.-a). About the Center for Energy Regulation & Policy Analysis. Retrieved July 8, 2021, from http://www.uwyo.edu/ser/research/centers-of-excellence/energy-regulation-policy/about.html

Center for Energy Regulation and Policy Analysis. (n.d.-b). People at the Center for Energy Regulation & Policy Analysis. Retrieved July 8, 2021, from https://www.uwyo.edu/ser/research/centers-of-excellence/energy-regulation-policy/people.html

Center for Energy Regulation and Policy Analysis. (n.d.-c). Welcome to the Center for Energy Regulation & Policy Analysis. Retrieved July 8, 2021, from http://www.uwyo.edu/ser/research/centers-of-excellence/energy-regulation-policy/index.html

H, Krutka (n.d.). About Us. Retrieved July 8, 2021, from http://www.uwyo.edu/ser/about-us/

School of Energy Resources. (September 15, 2019). The University of Wyoming School of Energy Resources annual report FY 2019. Retrieved from http://www.uwyo.edu/ser/about-us/reports/final-draft-fy19-ser-annual-report.pdf#2019%20Annual%20Report

School of Energy Resources. (September 15, 2020a). The University of Wyoming School of Energy Resources annual report FY 2020. Retrieved from http://www.uwyo.edu/ser/_files/docs/annual-reports/fy20-ser-annual-report-final.pdf

School of Energy Resources. (December 3, 2020b). UW School of Energy Resources welcomes new researchers. Retrieved July 8, 2021, from https://uwenergyreview.wordpress.com/2020/12/03/uw-school-of-energy-resources-welcomes-new-researchers/

School of Energy Resources. (n.d.-a). Centers of excellence. Retrieved July 8, 2021, from http://www.uwyo.edu/ser/research/centers-of-excellence/

School of Energy Resources. (n.d.-b). Energy Innovation Center. Retrieved July 8, 2021, from http://www.uwyo.edu/ser/building/

School of Energy Resources. (n.d.-c). Past research programs. Retrieved July 8, 2021, from http://www.uwyo.edu/ser/research/past-research-programs/index.html

University of Wyoming. (2019). Facts: 2018–19 academic year. Retrieved from http://www.uwyo.edu/oia/_files/fact-book/factbook2018_web.pdf

University of Wyoming. (2021). Facts: 2020–21 academic year. Retrieved from https://www.uwyo.edu/oia/_files/fact-book/factbook.pdf

U.S. Energy Information Administration. (2021). Wyoming - state energy profile analysis. Retrieved July 8, 2021, from https://www.eia.gov/state/analysis.php?sid=WY

Chapter 3

Center of Excellence for Cybersecurity

Pamela Shortt

Forsyth Technical Community College is situated in Winston-Salem, North Carolina. The main campus and eight center locations serve the communities of Forsyth and Stokes counties. The college has been offering vocational education since 1960 and has expanded to over 200 degree, diploma, and certificate options in addition to corporate training, continuing education, and personal enrichment classes. More than 22,000 students participate in curriculum, workforce continuing education, and basic skills classes each year.

In 2015, Forsyth Tech was designated by the National Security Agency (NSA) and Department of Homeland Security (DHS) as one of the first community colleges in North Carolina to be a National Center of Academic Excellence in Cyber Defense 2-Year Education (CAE-2Y), and the college was so redesignated in 2019.

The CAE-2Y designation is an institutional designation; however, the faculty and staff within the Cybersecurity Center are responsible for upholding the CAE-2Y program requirements. Within five years, the Cybersecurity Center has expanded from an online presence to creating physical lab space within the Thomas H. Davis *i*TEC Center on the main campus of Forsyth Tech.

PURPOSE AND OPERATIONS

The Cybersecurity Center exists to help address the shortage of cybersecurity professionals; thereby, reducing the vulnerability of the nation's information infrastructure through higher education and research in cyber defense. The CAE-2Y designation has been instrumental in developing industry and educational partnerships, supporting research and new cyber initiatives, and creating and sharing information to enhance and promote an educated cyber workforce (Forsyth Technical Community College, 2021).

Shortly after receiving the CAE-2Y designation, Forsyth Tech was named as the CAE Regional Resource Center (CRRC) in 2016 for the Central Eastern region of the United States.

The CRRC responsibilities include supporting and collaborating with CAE designated schools within the region, providing professional development opportunities to faculty at CAE institutions, and supporting and mentoring colleges working toward CAE designation in the Candidates Program (Forsyth Technical Community College, 2021). Forsyth Tech was also awarded funds to implement a Cybersecurity K-12 Pathway Initiative in 2017 to develop awareness and interest in cybersecurity careers among students in elementary and secondary grade levels (Forsyth Technical Community College, 2017)

External Partnerships

Most recently, Forsyth Tech has partnered with CyberFlorida at the University of South Florida, under leadership efforts of the University of West Florida to form the Southeast Regional Hub for the Centers of Academic Excellence in Cybersecurity for the Southeast United States (University of West Florida, 2020). As a regional hub partner, Forsyth Tech's Cybersecurity Center supports efforts that promote collaboration, partnerships, and training to strengthen the cybersecurity community in the Southeast region.

Expanding on the experience and relationships developed through the Cybersecurity K-12 Pathway Initiative, Forsyth Tech has also joined the Carolina Cyber Network to advance cybersecurity awareness and curriculum for K-12 educators by developing a repository of resources and facilitating cyber workshops that increase teachers' knowledge and skills in cybersecurity-related fields. The goal of introducing cybersecurity to younger students through integrated curriculum is to build a robust talent pipeline sufficient to fill the projected skills gap.

Although the CAE-2Y designation requires integration of critical security principles and practices throughout the institution and across multiple disciplines, faculty and administration must select at least one academic program that aligns to specific knowledge units. Students who complete the designated program requirements receive a notation on their diploma indicating the credential was earned from a Center of Academic Excellence in Cybersecurity.

Hiring managers from industries and government agencies readily recognize CAE-2Y graduates' skills as being aligned with the nationally accepted NICE Cybersecurity Workforce Framework. Forsyth Tech has nine Information Technology (IT) programs, with the IT-Systems Security degree mapped to the CAE-2Y knowledge units. Two of the shared core courses within the IT programs establish a strong foundation in networking and security concepts and practices, and all IT faculty are committed to integrating cybersecurity principles throughout the various program options.

FACULTY, STAFF, AND STUDENTS

In 2014, the Thomas H. Davis *i*TEC Center launched the online presence of the Cybersecurity Center at Forsyth Tech. After becoming a CAE-2Y, enrollment began to increase in cybersecurity related programs; therefore, the Thomas H. Davis *i*TEC Center was restructured to enhance leadership and support capacity for growth.

An associate dean position was created to provide direction and oversight of the Thomas H. Davis *i*TEC and Cybersecurity Centers, the administration of the CAE-2Y designation, and management of related grants. An administrative assistant was also hired to support the associate dean in activity planning, developing and distributing partner communications, and maintaining CAE-2Y documentation.

Two department chairpersons provide academic leadership for the nine IT programs within the Thomas H. Davis *i*TEC Center. The department chairpersons work directly with the associate dean and program faculty to ensure program changes and activities comply and align with the CAE-2Y purpose and goals.

Forsyth Tech has fourteen full-time and fourteen part-time IT faculty, including two full-time and five part-time cybersecurity faculty. The restructure created capacity for cybersecurity program enrollment to reach over 130 students in Fall 2020, which represents 38 percent of all IT students (K. Osborne, personal communication, June 28, 2021).

Enrollment

Enrollment in Forsyth Tech's cybersecurity-related programs has more than doubled since 2015. Activities and collaboration with secondary schools has also increased the number of Career and College Promise (CCP) dual-enrolled participants and attracted more students to enter cybersecurity programs after high school graduation. The percentage of students under the age of 24 has risen from 23% to almost 46%, with the median student age falling from 33 years old to 25 years old (K. Osborne, personal communication, June 28, 2021).

Much work has been done to recruit diverse student populations into the cybersecurity-related fields such as working with local Girl Scouts troops and Crosby Scholars' African American Males Pursuing Educational Dreams (AAMPED) Program, yet at present, two-thirds of students enrolled in cybersecurity related programs are white and almost 78 percent are male (K. Osborne, personal communication, June 28, 2021).

OUTCOMES

As a Center of Academic Excellence in Cybersecurity, Forsyth Tech is committed to providing quality education for developing cyber professionals. The primary outcomes of the Cybersecurity Center are to create skilled educators, prepare a trained workforce, and serve as a regional leader in building a collaborative cybersecurity community. GenCyber summer camps have been effective at increasing cybersecurity knowledge and interest among K-12 teachers and students.

High School and Middle School Outreach

Almost 90 middle and high school students have participated in the 40-hour GenCyber camps since 2017 (D. Wesley, personal communication, February 11, 2020). Middle and high school teachers are employed as teaching assistants for the camps, and they help the lead instructors develop activities based on cybersecurity first principles. The camp experience and skills learned have inspired some teachers to develop cyber clubs and activities within their area high schools (D. Wesley, personal communication, February 11, 2020).

To expand the cybersecurity community, Forsyth Tech has mentored colleges toward their CAE designation and has recruited other CAE institutions to join the mentor program. In 2018, Forsyth Tech hosted a CAE applicant and mentor workshop (Forsyth Technical Community College-Davis iTEC Center, 2017). As part of the Southeast CAE-C Regional Hub, Forsyth Tech plays a key role in expanding strategic partnerships to form a collaborative cybersecurity community (University of West Florida, 2020).

The robust and diverse cybersecurity advisory board, including leaders from the NC Department of Information Technology, biotechnology, and information technology fields provide valuable insight regarding local and state trends that impact cybersecurity curriculum development

Workforce Needs

Centers of Academic Excellence in Cybersecurity are critical to addressing the nation's need for qualified educators and a skilled workforce. North Carolina is among the top five states for cybersecurity jobs (Morgan, 2019), and it is "predicted to be second fastest growing tech state in the next five years" (NC TECH, 2021b, Opportunities section). Although North Carolina has the second highest percentage of women in the IT workforce at 35.4% (NC TECH, 2021b), Forsyth Tech will need to increase efforts to recruit females for cybersecurity programs to further narrow the gender gap among IT professionals.

Additionally, IT workers who identify as white fill 70 percent of the occupations, yet they represent only 63% of NC's population (NC TECH, 2021b). The average salary for a cybersecurity professional in North Carolina is over $100,000 (Morgan, 2019). Providing educational pathways for high-paying, successful cybersecurity careers is one of many ways Forsyth Tech promotes its vision of being "a catalyst for equitable economic mobility, empowering lives and transforming communities" (Forsyth Tech, p. 2, 2020).

STRENGTHS AND OPPORTUNITIES

As a CAE-2Y institution, Forsyth Tech employs highly qualified cybersecurity faculty committed to the standards of academic excellence established by the National Centers of Excellence in Cybersecurity. Many higher education institutions struggle to offer competitive industry wages compared to the private sector which adds to the complexities in recruiting and retaining full-time cybersecurity faculty in a market with an insufficient supply of workers. IT and cybersecurity are constantly changing.

Being connected with regional and national CAE partners provides access to valuable professional development opportunities and curriculum resources for faculty.

Although more people are entering IT and cybersecurity, the number of positions and job openings continue to grow which creates an ever-widening gap in the workforce. According to *Cybercrime Magazine*, there has been zero percent unemployment in the cybersecurity field since 2011(Morgan, 2019). Cybersecurity skills permeate through every job and role in the IT field. A major challenge to addressing the workforce needs is the length of time it takes to educate and equip individuals with the knowledge and skills needed to meet industry need.

Job Entry Requirements

More than 86% of North Carolina's entry-level IT jobs require a bachelor's degree or higher (NC TECH, 2021a). The CAE-2Y designation enables hiring managers to easily identify Forsyth Tech graduates earning an associate's degree who have met nationally recognized competencies necessary for employment based on the Workforce Framework for Cybersecurity which promotes easier access and earlier entry to employment.

Employers also look for national, industry-recognized certifications to select candidates with specific skills. Many courses within the IT and cybersecurity programs at Forsyth Tech prepare students for in-demand credentials such as the CompTIA Security+ certification. Students and community members can take certification exams on campus in the Davis *i*TEC Testing Center. More public-private collaboration is needed to reduce the time of entry into the workforce through efforts such as work-based learning and internship opportunities.

Options for Students

Forsyth Tech offers many options and pathways for students to help them achieve success in the manner that fits their needs. College and career fairs, summer camps, and campus events promote awareness among middle school and high school students about the exciting career opportunities in cybersecurity. Prospective students can choose from thirteen different IT certificates to complete while in high school.

Tuition is waived for high school students through the Career and College Promise dual enrollment program, so students can explore career pathways with minimal cost. For graduates interested in pursuing a bachelor's degree, Forsyth Tech has transfer articulation agreements with universities to accept the Associate in Applied Science degree course credits.

VALUE ADDED

The mission of Forsyth Tech is to advance "student success through excellence in learning, completion, equity, and post-graduation outcomes" (Forsyth Tech, 2020, p. 2). Hands-on experiential learning exercises are critical in fulfilling this mission. Students benefit from diverse learning labs including a Mac lab, Cisco Networking lab, Security Operations Center lab, and IT Skills lab.

In addition to working with physical devices to create secure networks, students practice skills online through the NETLAB+ remote access solution. Providing remote access to learning labs reduces barriers for students who may not be able to attend class or complete assignments on campus.

Equipment

The IT Skills lab is a collaborative space with iMacs, Windows laptops for checkout, pods to create networks, and small workgroup areas. The lab is open at least 20 hours a week for walk-in traffic. Every IT faculty member schedules at least one student hour each week to work in the lab and assist students. Work-study students are also scheduled to work in the lab as needed. When the lab is not opened for walk-in traffic, faculty can reserve the IT Skills lab for student class presentations or team meetings. Industry and community groups can also reserve the space for meetings, presentations, or training events.

The Security Operations Center lab opened in 2019, providing students and industry partners a lab for threat detection and incident response training (D. Wesley, personal communication, March 10, 2021). The lab is also equipped with virtual reality devices that are used to create immersive journeys for various innovative activities, interdisciplinary collaboration, and career exploration.

Funding for the lab furniture, equipment, and software was provided through various sources including a Department of Education Fund for the Improvement of Postsecondary Education (FIPSE) grant, Carl D. Perkins fund, and the Forsyth Tech Foundation.

Although the work at community colleges typically aligns with practical application of skills rather than research studies and publication, as a Center of Academic Excellence, Forsyth Tech supports cybersecurity research efforts, including developing and distributing resources to advance cyber education. Cybersecurity students have presented their research at national conferences for organizations such as the Women in CyberSecurity.

Additionally, Forsyth Tech is a partner in the NC STEM Alliance which provides opportunities for students from underrepresented groups in programs such as cybersecurity to become Research Fellows and receive mentoring by faculty. Elevating the importance of research in the Associate in Applied Science degree programs better prepares students for success in bachelor's studies and beyond. Additionally, projects such as the Equity Transfer Initiative with Winston-Salem State University is important for developing seamless transfer pathways for students in high demand programs such as IT and cybersecurity.

The main outcome for the initiative is "to increase transfer rates for African-American, Hispanic, adult and first-generation learners"

(Parham, 2021, para. 1). Providing pathways and reducing barriers to advanced degrees at a local university may also increase the likelihood of students remaining in the community after graduation; thereby, adding value to the local economy and workforce.

FUTURE OF EXCELLENCE

As many employees transitioned to working from home during the COVID-19 pandemic in 2020, malicious activity soared through phishing scams, ransomware attacks, and other methods that preyed on the vulnerabilities within organizations scrambling to continue operations without a playbook. New methods of attacks increased from 20% to 35% during the pandemic, including sophisticated attacks through machine learning and phone scams (Nabe, 2021).

Free community shredding events hosted by Forsyth Tech's Cybersecurity Center to encourage proper disposal of data stored on digital media and physical documents has been well received in the past and is increasingly important for remote workers who may unintentionally expose data to dumpster divers. Forsyth Tech will continue performing a critical role in bringing awareness and educating the community about the strategies bad actors use to collect personal information and access computer systems and data with malicious intent.

The college has offered an annual PC Diagnostic Clinic each year during which students work alongside instructors to perform system updates, virus removal, file system cleanup, and install antivirus software on personal computers and digital devices for community members. As clients wait for the service to be completed, they can participate in activities led by faculty to learn skills to protect their data and how to maintain optimal performance for their digital devices.

The clinic has served hundreds of community members since the inaugural event in 2016 (D. Wesley, personal communication, March 9, 2020). In the future, expanding partnership and collaboration with continuing education and workforce and economic development classes and services would increase the reach to more individuals in the community to increase digital competence and security practices.

Concern for Cybersecurity

Cybersecurity is a growing concern for every industry, especially as more systems are automated and globally connected. Manufacturing, financial, healthcare, and educational institutions are among the most vulnerable to cyber-attacks, and the cost of cybercrime is expected to rise to $10.5 trillion by 2025 (Business Advice & Research, 2021). Artificial Intelligence (AI) is gaining ground and will play a critical role in the future of cyber warfare.

AI can predict human response and penetrate through vulnerabilities at incredible rates; therefore, organizations will need to match the technology in combatting threats and reducing the response time for recovery. All Centers of Academic Excellence in Cybersecurity must constantly update curriculum and programs to prepare the current and future generation of cyber warriors.

Future Directions

Forsyth Tech faculty are exploring other programs such as Data Analytics and Reporting that can be aligned with the CAE knowledge units so more graduates are prepared to protect and defend the nation's technology infrastructure across various IT career paths. Curriculum is evolving to further integrate top skills such as secure application development, cloud security, and analysis. "Currently, jobs that require cloud security skills stay open for an average of 79 days. That is longer than virtually all IT job openings" (Guercio, 2020, para. 21).

Information security analyst positions are expected to grow at a higher rate than all other occupations, at 32 percent through 2028 (Guercio, 2020). Increasing internship and apprenticeship options for students will help reduce the time to job entry and narrow the gap in filling high demand positions.

CONCLUSION

Winston-Salem is home to six higher educational institutions; therefore, residents have many options to find the right fit for their academic and career goals. Forsyth Tech's core values of excellence, learning, innovation, diversity, and integrity (Forsyth Tech, 2020) sustain the operations and outcomes of its CAE-2Y designation. Partnerships with primary and secondary school systems, business and industries, and other post-secondary institutions are critical to building a robust workforce for cybersecurity careers.

The nation is at a critical point in which cybersecurity skills must be integrated across multiple disciplines such that security is part of everyone's job rather than residing just in the IT department of organizations. As a Center of Academic Excellence in Cybersecurity, Forsyth Tech faculty will continue leading efforts in elevating cyber awareness and personal responsibility throughout the community and beyond IT-focused programs of study with advanced technology and collaborative learning spaces.

REFERENCES

Business Advice & Research. (April 1, 2021). *2021 Must-know cyber attack statistics and trends*. Retrieved July 3, 2021, from Embroker: https://www.embroker.com/blog/cyber-attack-statistics/

Forsyth Tech. (2020). *Vision 2025*. Retrieved June 30, 2021, from Forsyth Tech: http://www.forsythtech.edu/files/discover/Vision+2020+Strategic+Plan.pdf?x15620

Forsyth Technical Community College. (March 23, 2017). *College Gets NSA Designation, Funding*. Retrieved June 26, 2021, from Forsyth Tech Magazine: https://www.forsythtech.edu/college-gets-nsa-designation-funding/#more-11851

Forsyth Technical Community College. (2021). *Davis iTEC Cyber Security Center*. Retrieved June 17, 2021, from Forsyth Tech: https://www.forsythtech.edu/davis-itec-cyber-security-center/

Forsyth Technical Community College-Davis iTEC Center. (2017). Retrieved June 17, 2021, from CAE Southeastern Regional Hub: https://crrc.forsythtech.edu/

Guercio, K. (2020, December 18). *Cybersecurity employment outlook 2021*. Retrieved July 5, 2021, from eSecurity Planet: https://www.esecurityplanet.com/trends/cybersecurity-employment-2021/

Morgan, S. (October 24, 2019). *Cybersecurity talent crunch to create 3.5 million unfilled jobs globally by 2021*. Retrieved July 1, 2021, from Cybercrime Magazine: https://cybersecurityventures.com/jobs/

Nabe, C. (2021). *Impact of COVID-19 on cybersecurity*. Retrieved July 3, 2021, from Deloitte: https://www2.deloitte.com/ch/en/pages/risk/articles/impact-covid-cybersecurity.html

NC TECH. (2021a). *Education and Automation*. Retrieved July 1, 2021, from NC State of Technology 2021 Industry Report: https://www.ncstir.com/tech-report/tech-occupations/education-automation/

NC TECH. (2021b). *Key Takeaways*. Retrieved July 1, 2021, from NC State of Technology 2021 Industry Report: https://www.ncstir.com/tech-report/key-takeaways-summary/

Parham, M. (January 21, 2021). *Equity transfer initiative aims to increase completion for minority students*. Retrieved July 2, 2021, from AACC: https://www.aacc.nche.edu/2021/01/21/equity-transfer-initiative-aims-to-increase-completion-for-minority-students/

University of West Florida. (December 2, 2020). *UWF re-designated as cybersecurity regional hub for the southeast US with expanded mission, region and partnerships*. Retrieved June 18, 2021, from Newsroom: https://news.uwf.edu/uwf-re-designated-as-cybersecurity-regional-hub-for-the-southeast-us-with-expanded-mission-region-and-partnerships/

Chapter 4

Center of Excellence for Biotechnology

Diana Cavender Dymek

Alamance Community College (ACC) is located in the county of Alamance, North Carolina with a main campus located in Graham, NC along with a secondary campus in Burlington, NC. Alamance is a two-year community college that offers over 35-degree, diploma, and certificate curriculum programs of study in business, arts, science, industrial technologies, and health and public services.

Alamance has a student body of 5,000, offering traditional technical courses as well as biotechnology, culinary technology, medical laboratory technology, and a host of university transfer courses. Alamance also offers distance learning, Career and College Promise, GED/Adult High School, job placement, workforce development, occupational extension, and personal enrichment.

Alamance was founded in 1958. As one of the first organized community colleges in North Carolina, the Burlington-Alamance County Industrial Education Center (IEC) signified a change in the landscape of education. It became Alamance Community College on January 1, 1988 and has continued to experience significant growth as it remains responsive to the educational, occupational, and cultural needs of the community.

A half century later, ACC continues to reinvent itself to fit the demands of an ever-changing workplace and the needs of 21st century students. Alamance Community College has a $200 million economic impact each year on Alamance County and its cutting-edge programs reflect the newest career and job opportunities for Alamance's students (Alamance Community College, 2021).

In addition, this author interviewed faculty, staff, trustees, students, and researched information about the Biotechnology COE shared by Alamance Community College. Lastly, research was completed related to the biotechnology industry in North Carolina and biotechnology industry trends specific to the Triad and Piedmont regions of North Carolina (Y. Butler (personal communication, May 12, 2021).

BACKGROUND OF A CENTER OF EXCELLENCE

Alamance Community College is a high-tech hub for workforce development, for jobs skills training, and for scientific collaboration across the Triad and Triangle areas of North Carolina. According to President A. Gatewood, five years ago, with the help of community leaders, Alamance imagined a Center of Excellence (COE). Today, ACC is laying the foundation for that bold vision. Construction on the $17.6 million Biotechnology Center of Excellence began in May 2021 with plans to open Fall 2022, transforming ACC and advancing economic development in the county and across the region.

ACC is building on its reputation as a statewide leader and innovator in the rapidly growing field of biotechnology, histotechnology, agriculture biotechnology, medical and laboratory technology, and related life and physical sciences (A. Gatewood, personal communication May 12, 2021).

College Board Action

In 2015, the college's board of trustees proposed establishing a COE. By early 2016, the college had assembled a commission to review expert analysis, data, and forecast economic trends. That commission represented government, education, business, healthcare, and the non-profit sectors. Through a series of roundtable discussions, ideas for a COE were proposed and vetted.

The college's longstanding biotechnology program emerged as a major strength upon which to build. The broad-based commission support and feedback was vital to this project but no less vital was Alamance's $39.6 million education bond referendum in 2018 of which the Biotechnology COE was the centerpiece.

Today, a new group of community leaders is helping guide the decision making and strategy of designing the COE and deploying its technologies. For more than five years, the college has relied on community collaboration and feedback to turn a dream into a reality (R. Crisp, personal communication, May 12, 2021).

Purpose of a Biotechnology Center of Excellence

A center of excellence leverages an expertise vital to regional business and industry. It identifies a unique program or cluster of programs critical to job skills training and workforce development. In turn, the center of excellence becomes an economic driver in a region of the state. Generally speaking, the programs in the center of excellence are widely regarded as an existing strength in the college.

That strength is one that is highly specialized and not easily replicated by nearby community colleges. A community college center of excellence should lend itself to partnerships and collaborations with area business, industry, and even academic and research centers. At ACC, biotechnology and related life sciences programs were identified as a unique strength (Mr. Y. Butler, personal communication, May 12, 2021).

According to Dr. Bridget Ledford Waters, Department Head of Medical Laboratory Technicians/Histotechnology, the college has the largest running two-year biotechnology program in the nation. ACC has one of the most complete biomanufacturing suites of any North Carolina college and the college's cell culture program is second to none in equipment, facilities, and students work with state-of-the art stem cell and tissue engineering technologies. Because of this, the college is forging strong partnerships and collaborations with local business and industry across the Triad and Triangle.

This has brought business support and donations of state-of-the-art equipment to the college. The college's biotechnology and life sciences programs have long enjoyed a reputation for innovation and expertise. It has long been recognized as a respected leader in a central piedmont region. ACC is poised to enjoy a new role as a statewide leader as its center of excellence takes shape in life sciences, job skills training, and research collaboration (B L. Waters, personal communication, May 12, 2021).

WHAT IS BIOTECHNOLOGY?

Many everyday products, such as coffee filters, cleaners, detergents, cat litter, and hygiene products are the work of biotechnology. Many of the foods that are consumed such as breakfast cornflakes, canola oil, bread, cheese, and lactose free milk are the work of biotechnology. It is estimated that nearly 75% of the processed foods in a grocery store are impacted by biotechnology.

Biotechnology uses living organisms to perform specific industrial or manufacturing processes. Biotechnology leverages nature and its cellular and molecular processes to develop new products. Biomanufacturing is the part of biotechnology that brings these critical new products to the world.

Medical Applications

Many diagnostic technologies and therapeutics are the end-product of biotechnology. Biotechnology is used to battle breast cancer, leukemia, diabetes, heart disease, HIV, MS, arthritis, hepatitis, Alzheimer's Disease. It is also involved in vaccines and antibiotics. When filling up at gas pumps, biotechnology is leveraged. When law enforcement gathers DNA, biotechnology is used.

Farmers use it to battle drought, pests, and fungi. In a world of exploding populations, plant and cropland is shrinking. Biotechnology holds the key to delivering greater food yields in less space. Biotechnology heals, feeds, and fuels the world (Alamance Community College, 2021).

Biotechnology Center of Excellence Operations and Programs

Synergies exist when related life and physical science programs come together at Alamance. The COE invites collaboration among biotechnology and three other programs such as medical laboratory technology, histotechnology, and agricultural biotechnology.

Medical Laboratory Technology Program

Medical laboratory technology students learn to perform clinical laboratory test procedures on blood and bodily fluids. These tests help in diagnosis of conditions such as diabetes, heart disease, and cancer. These tests help guide treatment options for healthcare providers and their patients. The medical laboratory technology program is over 30 years old and one of the longest such programs in North Carolina (Alamance Community College, 2021).

Histotechnology Program

In histotechnology, ACC students learn to prepare and process tissue samples for examination and diagnosis by pathologists. The program places graduates on the frontlines of diagnostic and treatment strategies. Histotechnology is one of the most recent additions to the academic program. There is a regional and national shortage of technologists in histotechnology and also medical laboratory technologists according to a 2019 Scientific American Report (Alamance Community College, 2021).

Agricultural Biotechnology Program

Agricultural biotechnology prepares students to enter the industry focused on areas of research in plant production utilizing biochemistry, genetics, microbiology, and cell culture. This specialty area was also recently added at ACC, is the only one of its kind in North Carolina, and is linked to the horticulture technology program which focuses on plant science, plant materials, and plant production.

The horticulture program enjoys a close relationship with the culinary arts program which is often the recipient of the end products from horticulture. Additionally, culinary students focus on food safety, sanitation, and science—all with practical applications to biotechnology (Alamance Community College, 2021).

IT and Mechatronics Programs

IT and mechatronics programs are also part of the COE at ACC. Any manufacturing industry would be hard pressed to operate without the software and hardware skills of information technologists. These workers design and manage information systems—particularly in such specialized areas as healthcare informatics, bioinformatics, and mechatronics engineering technology.

This nexus of computer, mechanical, and electrical engineering is critical across a wide range of industry, particularly those that rely on robotics to manufacture large quantities of a particular product. IT and mechatronics are part of the collaboration envisioned at the Biotechnology COE. Soon, it is envisioned that food sciences will join the constellation of existing programs (B. L. Waters, personal communication, May 12, 2021).

The COE is meant to leverage partnerships and collaborations with biopharmaceutical companies, diagnostic centers, hospitals, and agricultural research centers. These are in rich abundance across the Central Piedmont of North Carolina. One of the largest running academic-private industry partnerships which Alamance Community College has maintained is with LabCorp, the world's largest diagnostic company, and its headquarters in Alamance County. The biotechnology, histotechnology, and medical laboratory programs have enjoyed a great deal of success because of this important partnership.

LabCorp employs many of the graduates. It is a strong contributor to the college's foundation. In recent years, LabCorp has twice been named ACC's Business Partner of the Year. Additional business partners include: FlexCell International, Avgol, Eurofins Scientific, Syngenta, Siemens, Anderson Sterilizers, Inc., Carolina Biological Supply, BD Diagnostics, Cone Health, The North Carolina Biotechnology Center, The Golden Leaf Foundation, UNC system universities, and the Joint School of Nanoscience and Nanoengineering (Alamance Community College, 2021).

Building Layout

The COE has a modern design with ample, exterior glass meant to stand out as a landmark and also a gateway for the college and Alamance County. It is a three-story building with approximately 30,000 square feet, state of the art teaching labs, classrooms, student areas, outdoor learning spaces, and offices. There will be naming rights opportunities for business partners visible to more than 100,000 interstate travelers on I-40 each day.

The second floor is anticipated to host conferences, meetings, and community events in addition to the academic programs. An outside learning area will be able to also host events for students and the community. The building is designed for maximum flexibility and further expansion (Y. Butler, personal communication, May 12, 2021).

Biotechnology Center of Excellence Faculty, Staff, and Students

Students furthering their education in biotechnology at ACC have a number of different pathways available to them and courses are taught by instructors with real world biotechnology experience. There is a certificate option so that students may learn biotechnology basics in as little as one semester to become certified to begin employment in bioinformatics technology or laboratory technology. There is a diploma program to allow completion in half the time of the two-year degree program so that students may take a variety of classes so as to help them gain all the skills needed to be successful.

There is also the deepest dive into biotechnology with a two-year Associate in Applied Sciences degree in order to gain exposure in all areas of biology, chemistry, math, and communications in order to begin a career in the industry (Alamance Community College, 2021).

Alamance students in the Biotechnology COE enter the college with different backgrounds including: first generation students, military veterans, students with other bachelor degrees, those seeking an associate degree on their journey to earning a bachelor degree, and certificate and diploma seeking students. Many students enter the workforce directly upon graduation and many have employment offers prior to program completion.

Students learn from faculty and staff who have worked in the field and are able to work closely with faculty and staff as the class sizes are smaller than most universities. Classrooms in the new Biotechnology COE building will have a maximum capacity of 24 students. Opportunities also exist for students to work with industry partners through internship positions which can also lead to full-time employment possibilities (Alamance Community College, 2021).

Value of the Biotechnology Center of Excellence to the Students and Service Area

Alamance County voters approved a $39.6 million bond referendum in 2018 which made the Biotechnology Center of Excellence possible as the citizens recognized the importance to the college, Alamance County, and the state of North Carolina. The bioscience job growth projections boast a trajectory and economic future seldom seen in career fields. These are jobs in stable, well-paying fields such as biotechnology, medical laboratory technology, agricultural biotechnology, and histotechnology. The median salaries are $40,000 to $50,000 annually. Those income levels are higher than the median salaries of the average Alamance County.

Ripple Effect

That has an economic ripple effect across the county. The life sciences employees are boosting the county's tax base and contributing to the economic vitality of the area. A key factor in business and industry recruitment and retention is the resources and workforce development expertise a community college can provide. Business recruitment and retention is the lifeblood of a county's wellbeing. When a city's tax base is growing, business is thriving, and the public education system is flourishing, social and public health safety sectors are less pressured, and the overall standard of living is improved.

The North Carolina Biotechnology Center is a valued partner of the college and shares in the continued growth in North Carolina biomanufacturing industry which will require new employees with complex training and technical skills. Close to 2,500 new employees will be needed in the biopharmaceutical manufacturing industries while fewer than 200–300 workers are currently trained annually. A skills gap is being bridged and paramount to Alamance's wellbeing (C. Wolfe, personal communication, May 12, 2021).

FUTURE VALUE OF THE BIOTECHNOLOGY COE TO THE INSTITUTION'S SERVICE AREA

From 2014 to 2019, the growth rate of bioscience jobs in Alamance County doubled from 1,982 jobs to 3,948 jobs. Growth rate across the Piedmont Triad grew 37%. During the same time, total economic impact of bioscience industry in North Carolina had increased 60% and was estimated to be $73 billion in 2014. By 2025, the economic impact of biosciences in North Carolina is projected to top $100 billion (North Carolina Biotechnology Center, 2021). North Carolina is third in the nation in its biosciences footprint and there are more than 650 life sciences companies in the state employing more than 66,000 workers.

Burlington, NC is the nation's number one small metropolitan statistical area for research testing and medical labs. Alamance County is home to the world's largest healthcare diagnostics company, LabCorp. It is also home to the nation's leading supplier of science teaching materials, Carolina Biological Supply Company. Alamance Community College is positioned both geographically and strategically in North Carolina's most active biotechnology corridor (Piedmont Triad Regional Council, 2021).

Nestled between the Triad (the region in North Carolina anchored by three cities: Greensboro, Winston-Salem, and High Point) with the Triangle metropolitan markets and Research Triangle Park, metropolitan area in the Piedmont region of North Carolina, all of which is anchored by three major research universities: North Carolina State University, Duke University, and University of North Carolina at Chapel Hill, ACC is at the epicenter of an exciting economical chapter in North Carolina's history (Research Triangle Park, 2021).

FUTURE OF THE BIOTECHNOLOGY CENTER OF EXCELLENCE

Future business partners for the COE may include: Pfizer, University of North Carolina, Merck, Biogen, BASF, Wake Health, Kbi Biopharma, Cooks Medical Devices, Novazyme, and Wake Forest Institute of Regenerative Medicine. The college and Biotechnology COE finds itself at the epicenter of a robust life sciences industrial constellation (B L. Waters, personal communication, May 12, 2021).

The COE's approximate 11,000 square feet third floor is intentionally planned to be shell space for future labs and classes, intended for future expansion, technology not yet envisioned, new programs, and partnerships not yet developed. Additionally, a research greenhouse can be built if there is identification of additional funds beyond initial Biotechnology COE needs. It is expected to have four research areas, two will host bio agriculture students, others will be reserved for collaboration among faculty, students, and external partners (Y. Butler, personal communication, May 12, 2021.

In addition, the recent launch of the agricultural biotechnology program has generated much attention from several prospective business partners across North Carolina's agricultural biotechnology community regarding potential collaborations (Alamance Community College, 2021).

CONCLUSION

A community college center of excellence should lend itself to partnerships and collaborations with area business, industry, and even academic and research centers. At Alamance Community College, the strengths in its biotechnology and related life sciences programs led to just such a center of excellence.

The ACC Biotechnology Center of Excellence is poised to advance economic development in the county and across the region. The Biotechnology COE builds on its reputation as a statewide leader and innovator in the rapidly growing field of biotechnology, histotechnology, agriculture biotechnology, medical and laboratory technology, and related life and physical sciences.

REFERENCES

Alamance Community College (2021). Retrieved from http://alamancecc.edu
North Carolina Biotechnology Center (2021). Retrieved from https://www.ncbiotech.org
Piedmont Triad Regional Council (2021). Retrieved from https://www.ptrc.org/services/economic-development
Research Triangle Park (2021). Retrieved from https://www.rtp.org

Chapter 5

Center of Excellence for Business

Roy E. Allen

Saginaw Valley State University's history dates to 1922 with the formation of the first area college: Bay City Junior college, which eventually became Delta College in 1961. To meet the four-year baccalaureate program desire, Saginaw Valley College was founded as a private institution in November 1963. In 1965, the college became a state-supported institution. In 1974, Saginaw Valley College changed its name to Saginaw Valley State College and again to Saginaw Valley State University (SVSU) in 1987.

Located in Saginaw County, Michigan, halfway between Saginaw and Bay City, SVSU offers more than 100 academic undergraduate and graduate programs of study. Ranked 119th best college by the U. S. News & World Report in 2021, SVSU boasts an enrollment of 8,265 students with an in-state tuition rate of $10,814 (Saginaw Valley State University, 2021).

"Saginaw Valley is an absolutely first-class University! It is clean, the atmosphere of the campus is very welcoming and relaxed. . ." (2021 Best College Campuses in America, 2021, p. 1). The College of Business is among the programs of study at SVSU's five colleges. Niche ranked Business as the second most popular major at SVSU (2021 Best College Campuses in America, 2021).

SCOTT L. CARMONA COLLEGE OF BUSINESS

Scott L. Carmona is a business graduate of Saginaw Valley State College from the early '70s and owner of Sunrise National Distributors Inc., a leading regional wholesale distributor of automotive accessories. A successful business entrepreneur with businesses along the I-75 corridor from Michigan to Florida, Scott and his family pledged "the lead gift for the fundraising campaign for SVSU's business school" (News, 2018, p. 1).

Completed in 2020, a new 38,500 square foot building, at the cost of $25.4 million, opened its doors as the primary facility for the Scott L. Carmona School of Business (MLive Media Group, 2020). Housed in the Carmona building, wholly or in part, are five business centers forming the Business Excellence Center—Scott L. Carmona College of Business.

BUSINESS EXCELLENCE CENTERS

Saginaw Valley State University's Business Excellence Center (BEC) is a collection of 5 centers: The Stevens Center for Family Business, The Dow Entrepreneurship Institute, The Michigan Manufacturing Technology Center, The Independent Testing Laboratory, and The Small Business Development Center.

According to Doctor Izabella Szymanska, Associate Professor of Management and acting Director, The Dow Entrepreneurship, SVSU is a teaching-focused university. The Business Excellence Centers provide opportunities for students to excel. However, the centers are equally rooted in providing similar opportunities for the local communities (I. Szymanska, personal communication, May 25, 2021).

The Stevens Center for Family Business

In existence for more than 22 years, the Stevens Center for Family Business (SCFB) nurtures Michigan businesses by providing "major event series, membership programs, and academic coursework in family business" (Stevens Center for Family Business, 2021, p. 1). The event series sponsors nationally recognized experts in areas of family businesses at significant events. The speakers focus on issues confronted by family-owned businesses and firms.

Notable presenters have included the owners of Bronner's CHRISTmas Wonderland and Frankenmuth Bavarian Inn, two globally recognized travel destinations in Michigan. At the cost of $500 or less, annually, family and family-firm memberships offer unlimited participation in all event-sponsored activities of the SCFB.

The Dow Entrepreneurship Institute

Funded by the Herbert H. & Grace A. Dow Foundation, the Dow Entrepreneurship Institute (DEI) is synonymous with creating local businesses in Michigan. Much of the Institute's work enriches students and local businesses by offering various events for student participation. The events are aimed at business innovation and provide student internships for local companies and students. (I. Szymanska, personal communication, May 25, 2021).

The elevator pitch is among the most popular Institute events. Students prepare and deliver an elevator pitch in 120 seconds or less. The business must be owned at least 50% by a student, and the business's previous year's sales must be greater than $200,000. The prize is $2,000 in funding and the thrill of the competition.

The Institute is rather eclectic, requiring various equipment to bring entrepreneur's prototypes to life. The Institute possesses, among other things, a welder, a top-of-the-line sewing machine, fabric printers, and 3D printers in brand new maker's space in the Carmona building. Maker space provides the community and students a location and business development resources to experiment with various manufacturing tools and techniques (I. Szymanska, personal communication, May 25, 2021).

The Michigan Manufacturing Technology Center

The Michigan Manufacturing Technology Center (MMTC) has been in existence for more than 30 years. Still, a state-wide initiative five years ago developed a regional strategic partnership plan for workforce agencies, governmental agencies, businesses and manufacturers, and colleges. The regional partnership, or regionalism, results from the Detroit

Regional Chamber of Commerce (DRCC) influence. The DRCC is one of the oldest and most influential Chamber of Commerce boards in the nation and publishes an annual comprehensive and authoritative State of the Region economics report (Who we are, 2021).

The Chamber secured a building to house the Small Business Center, The Michigan Economic Center, and various workforce agencies to perform business and manufacturing research. The federal government recognized the center's success and influenced regionalism collaboration across the state (J. Bockelman, personal communication, May 24, 2021).

Government influence resulted in the development of the Michigan Manufacturing Technology Center of Excellence at SVSU. The MMTC provides consulting services to Michigan manufacturers over an eleven-county area in Central Northeast Michigan. Consulting services include: Cybersecurity, Growth, Operational excellence, Leadership development, Skill development, Advanced technology, Research services, and Food processing.

The MMTC provides comprehensive and affordable consulting services to evaluate and train manufacturing employees and management on manufacturing techniques designed to optimize production results (J. Bockelman, personal communication, May 24, 2021).

The Independent Testing Laboratory

Housed in SVSU's College of Science, Engineering, and Technology, The Independent Testing Laboratory offers testing and research & development (R&D) for hundreds of Michigan manufacturers and companies. The laboratory is a fully equipped independent testing laboratory offering mechanical, chemical, and environmental testing and microscopy testing services. Benefits of using the laboratory include quicker product development, R&D-based design solutions, and significant knowledge and insight to solve complex business and manufacturing problems (Independent testing laboratory, 2021).

The Small Business Development Center

Michigan's Small Business Development Center (SBDC) "provides consulting, training, and research to assist small business to launch, grow, transition and motivate" (The small business development centers (SBDC), 2021, p. 1). In Michigan, the SBDC is a collection of eleven regional centers with the Northeast & Great Lakes Bay Region located in the SVSU's Carmona building.

Like the MMTC, the SBDC offers a robust array of services in business start-up, business growth, cybersecurity, business plan refinement, financial analysis and projections, and market research. Created in 2020, The Northeast & Great Lakes Bay Region includes 15 counties and stretches from Saginaw North to the Mackinac bridge (B Roszatycki, personal communication, May 24, 2021).

The prior regional SBDC host was Delta College. In 2019, the center moved to SVSU with the vision of developing strong community connections and providing a significant business resource to the community. The center offers transition, succession, and strategic planning, and experiential learning for students at no cost to clients. The SBDC is half-funded by SVSU and half from the Michigan Economic Corporation. Five metrics are used to measure the SBDC impact and success, the number of business start-ups, capital formation, jobs created/retained, contact hours with clients, and the number of trainings and workshops.

PEOPLE OF THE BUSINESS EXCELLENCE CENTER

The consulting/training nature of the five business centers equates to low direct faculty involvement. Many SVSU students use the Business Excellence Center, but the centers do not provide academic instruction, except for experiential learning. Academic instruction in areas of business and science, for instance, is augmented by the opportunities presented by the Business Excellence Center. Because SVSU is a clearinghouse of sorts, where the business centers are married to the community, the staff is generally limited to a director and an administrative assistant.

The Michigan Manufacturing Technology Center provides robust training seminars, consulting, and ongoing business development throughout the region. However, the instructors are neither faculty nor staff at SVSU. At the time of this research, the only MMTC employees were the director and the administrative assistant (J. Bockelman, personal communication, May 24, 2021).

The Scott L. Carmona College of Business provides more than ten extra-curricular activities and programs that utilize the Business Excellence Center. Students in accounting societies, marketing associations, and other organizations regularly use the BEC's resources for their projects.

THE IMPACT OF THE BUSINESS EXCELLENCE CENTER

The impact of the BEC is significant. For example, for every dollar a company spent at the MMTC, it returned 21 dollars in financial improvement. In providing metric success figures, over the last three years, the MMTC has been responsible for $108 million in new sales, $178 million in retained sales, $50.7 million in cost savings, $110 million investments made, and 1,915 jobs created (personal communication, J. Bockelman, May 24, 2021).

BUSINESS EXCELLENCE CENTER OUTCOMES

As previously mentioned, all five of the centers use metrics for success benchmarks and report similar outcomes. For a practical application of the center's results, the success of Dyna Products and the Ideal Party Store are exemplary.

Ideal Party Store

In 1934, Roy and Julia Crete opened the Ideal Party Store in Bay City, Michigan, immediately following the repeal of prohibition. Roy had a fifth-grade education, and his wife had an eighth-grade education. Over 87 years, the family built the local party store to a $6 million yearly income through hard work and the Stevens Center for Family Business support. Third-generation Ideal Party Store owner Jerry Crete says they are dues-paying members of the SBDC, which provides collaboration, training, and networking for like-minded business owners.

Jerry is a graduate of the local Delta College, a community college, and active in the local business community. Jerry also served on the Delta College Foundation Board, where during his membership, the foundation holdings grew from $20 million to over $34 million in eight years (J. Crete, personal communication June 15, 2021).

Dyna Products

Founded by twin brothers Norman and Nathan Miller in 1984, Dyna Products produces firewood processing machines. In 2019, Dyna Products approached the MMTC at SVSU about improving the efficiency of their manufacturing process. The MMTC reviewed the manufacturing process and made suggestions for manufacturing improvements using the LEAN business approach that completely changes how a business and employees think and act.

By moving from a batch production approach to a single piece flow method, Dyna Products is on track to increase its gross annual income from $6.2 million in 2019 to $10 million in 2021 with success credit to the MMTC (N. Miller, personal communication, June 15, 2021).

BUSINESS EXCELLENCE CENTER STRENGTHS AND WEAKNESSES

The overwhelming strength of the BEC is the collaborative nature of the individual centers housed in the BEC. Collaboration in the sense that the individual centers receive service, support, and direction from local and state organizations such as the Great Lakes Bay Manufacturers Association, Michigan Economic Development Corporation, Michigan Works, Delta College, and the Saginaw and Bay Area Chambers of Commerce. Providing students and local business entrepreneurs access to business training, consulting, and research in a one-stop shopping venue is a best practice approach other Excellence Centers should note.

Perhaps the most significant weakness of the BEC is the differing nature of business needs and students' needs. Successful businesses do not slow or stop. Development and growth are spurred by constant business practice evaluation, adaptation, and change. The University and students, on the other hand, slow and stop often.

Semester breaks, graduation, introducing new programs of study, and removing old programs of study all negatively impact businesses if they rely solely on student support for their consulting needs. However, this weakness enables the collaborative nature between the University and the BEC to be so successful (J. Bockelman, personal communication, May 24, 2021).

THE VALUE OF THE CENTER FOR THE STUDENTS

For SVSU students, the BEC is like having the most advanced, interactive laboratory that complements academic endeavors and provides a practical work-based learning experience. As part of the Scott L. Carmona College of Business, the BEC encourages student involvement in training, consulting, and providing research services to local businesses and manufacturers. Some students may be business owners or entrepreneurs themselves and utilize the BEC facilities and resources to develop their business model.

The centers support students from other academic disciplines as well. For instance, even though it is one of the five business centers of the BEC, the Independent Testing Laboratory is housed in the College of Science, Engineering, and Technology and encourages those students to take advantage of that resource (Independent testing laboratory, 2021).

AN ANALYSIS OF THE VALUE OF THE CENTER FOR THE INSTITUTION

Saginaw Valley State University's relationship with the Business Excellence Center is best characterized as a symbiotic relationship benefiting the University, the individual business centers, and the business community. From the institution's perspective, the University provides some facility space to house the business centers and contributes minimally to the overall employee salaries of the centers.

Comparatively speaking, the relationship is altruist in the sense that SVSU is a clearinghouse providing space and minimal financial investment for a collection of business centers responsible for billions of dollars of economic impact in their region. The MMTC's primary responsibility is not student education but rather federal and state contractual obligations to provide business and manufacturing consultation, development, and support (J. Bockelman, personal communication, May 24, 2021).

THE FUTURE OF THE BUSINESS EXCELLENCE CENTER

The future of SVSU's BEC is bright. In May, the University hired a new Dean of the Scott L. Carmona College of Business, Jayati Ghosh. Ghosh replaces the outgoing Dean who was the moving force resulting in the construction of the Scott L. Carmona building, and brings the air of revitalization for the BEC whose staff members are hopeful they can set up shop in the new Carmona building and increase collaborative efforts between the five centers and the University. Finally, Economic indicators are moving in a positive direction, which bodes well for the University, the Business Excellence Center, and the people of Michigan.

CONCLUSION

Saginaw Valley State University's Business Excellence Center is comprised of five business centers that comprehensively meet the student, business, and manufacturing needs of the area. The five centers operate independently under various federal and state guidelines while collaboratively providing services meeting SVSU's academic requirements. All five centers share similar success metrics revolving around education, contact, and collaboration with local businesses and manufacturers and improved economic development indicators demonstrating increased income, production, jobs created, and jobs retained.

The totality of services provided applies to small businesses such as the Ideal Party Store and large companies such as Dyna Products. One of the most significant strengths of the BEC is the support received from state and local agencies such as the Michigan Economic Development Corporation, Michigan Works, Delta College, and the Saginaw and Bay Area Chambers of Commerce. The center provides a robust array of services for students and businesses in a successful symbiotic relationship that is likely to continue well into the future.

REFERENCES

2021 Best College Campuses in America. (June 30, 2021). Retrieved from Niche: https://www.niche.com/colleges/search/best-college-campuses/

Independent testing laboratory. (May 24, 2021). Retrieved from Saginaw Valley State University: https://www.svsu.edu/itl/#

MLive Media Group. (February 24, 2020). Retrieved from YouTube: https://www.youtube.com/watch?v=PFFSJv3MXlE

News. (June 19, 2018). Retrieved from Saginaw Valley State University: https://www.svsu.edu/scottlcarmonacollegeofbusiness/news/4/

Saginaw Valley State University. (June 30, 2021). Retrieved from U.S. News: https://www.usnews.com/best-colleges/saginaw-valley-state-2314

Stevens Center for Family Business. (May 25, 2021). Retrieved from Saginaw Valley State University: https://www.svsu.edu/stevenscenterforfamilybusiness/aboutscfb/

The small business development centers (SBDC). (May 24, 2021). Retrieved from U. S. Small Business Administration: https://www.vetbizcentral.org/small-business-development-center/

Who we are. (May 24, 2021). Retrieved from Detroit Regional Chamber: https://www.detroitchamber.com/the-chamber/who-we-are/

Chapter 6

Center of Excellence for Agriculture and Water

Von Locklear

The Northeast Community College Agriculture and Water Center of Excellence is located in Norfolk, Nebraska and has a service area of twenty counties and 14,400 square miles with one main campus, three extended campuses, and two regional offices.

REVIEW OF THE SITUATION

This chapter will provide a background of Northeast Community College, describe how Northeast Community College determined that there was a necessity followed by a vision for the Agriculture and Water Center of Excellence, describe the funding for the Northeast Community College Agriculture & Water Center of Excellence, describe the Nexus, and describe the strengths and improvements projected to be made to the Center.

Background

The agriculture industry in northeast Nebraska accounts for fifty percent of the jobs. In addition, Nebraska is a leader in the United States beef and beef-related products, red meat, and popcorn production (College, 2019b). Further, Nebraska is a leader in the United States in the cattle and hay business and grain corn and other livestock. Students attending Northeast Community College learn and understand Nebraska's deep agricultural legacy while learning new advanced technology methods in different Agriculture, Food, and Natural Resources Programs ("The Nexus Capital Campaign," n.d.).

Northeast Community College has a five hundred acre working farmland adjacent to the college (T. Kruse, personal communication, June 02, 2021). Northeast Community College provides twelve programs of study including AgriBusiness (AAS), Agriculture-College Transfer (AA, AS), Agronomy (AAS), Animal Science (AAS), Dairy Technician (Diploma), Diversified Agriculture (AAS), Horticulture and Golf Course Management (AAS), Mechanized Agriculture (AAS), Natural Resources (AS), Precision Agriculture (AAS), Pre-Veterinary Technology (AS), and Veterinary Technology (AAS) (College, n.d.-a).

Vision and Necessity

The vision and necessity for the Northeast Community College Agriculture and Water Center of Excellence began in 2015 with a recommendation from a college advisory committee. This recommendation led to focus groups and surveys with over three hundred business and industrial leaders, employers, and students about Northeast Community College's need to address the current situation. Northeast Community College lacked adequate facilities to handle the Agriculture, Food, and Natural Resources Programs (T. Kruse, personal communication, June 02, 2021).

Most of the current facilities are approximately one hundred years old and obsolete. In addition, these facilities were unable to align will the proper needs of the students. The Veterinary Technology program was located in two facilities approximately one mile apart. The "faculty offices, one classroom, and a pathology class laboratory are currently located in 2,600 square feet of space in the Agriculture and Allied Health building on the main campus" (College, 2019a, para. 5). In addition, the Veterinary Technology program clinic is located in the approximately one hundred years old obsolete farm building.

Large Animal and Farm Operations Facility

This building is known as the Large Animal and Farm Operations (College, 2019a). Dr. Michael Chipps stated:

> As we examined the landscape of agriculture in Nebraska, we found a growing need to develop more agricultural producers and related industry personnel who understand how to use data and technology to make better decisions, produce higher yields and conserve our natural resources. In essence, it would be doing more with less to feed a hungry world. (College, 2016, para. 4)

As a result, Northeast Community College redesigned the programs offered at the college to allow a more reframed education environment focused on next-generation agriculture science (College, 2016). The vision for the Northeast Community College Agriculture and Water Center of Excellence is simple. The Center of Excellence envisions: "integrating innovation, demonstration, applied research and training that not only educates the next generation of producers and agriculture specialists, but correspondingly showcases this work to producers and business and industry partners" (College, 2016, para. 6).

Lastly, the vision of the Northeast Community College Agriculture and Water Center of Excellence is just not confined to the service area of Northeast Nebraska, but the vision includes making sustainable agriculture available to the world (T. Kruse, personal communication, June 02, 2021).

The Northeast Center of Excellence is set to open in two phases. Phase one will consist of the farm and livestock operations, large animal handling facility, veterinary technology, and precision and mechanized agriculture. Phase two will consist of agriculture classrooms, agriculture complex expansion, greenhouse, innovation, and demonstration center, and programmatic support ("Phase I & II," n.d.).

PHASE ONE

In phase one, the farm and livestock operations will be updated. The current conditions of the farm and livestock operations prior to Fall 2021 are the barn is inadequate for the newer high-tech agriculture equipment and larger farm animals and larger class sizes; the space has inadequate ventilation for students, staff, faculty, and animals, the height of the ceilings are too low, and the layout is not conducive to learning and instruction.

The sheds do not have cement floors, lack electricity, have leaking rooftops and are too small for the modern high-tech agricultural machinery; the structures and feedlot have water drainage issues, and the design is not efficient and adds stress to the animals during movement, and handling ("College Farm and Livestock," n.d., para 2).

Ron Coufal, a local producer and member of the Northeast Agriculture Advisory Committee Member, stated the purpose of this need:

> It is critical that we improve the ag facilities at Northeast Community College and diversify the farming operation. This should include outdoor pens with a lagoon so that students can learn how to manage them. They also need to learn how to buy and sell cattle and get experience with all the different aspects of raising a healthy herd. Students will then take that knowledge back to their farms to be able to compete down the road. ("College Farm and Livestock," n.d., para. 4)

The Phase 1 updates will include larger structures for the high-tech agricultural machinery with an office; adequate space for student instruction; adequate space for the animals allowing for less stress during movement and handling, resulting in more hands-on training for the students; safer structures for the students, staff, faculty, and animals, and a well-drained feedlot allowing for hands-on training for the students ("College Farm and Livestock," n.d., para. 6).

Farm and Livestock Operations

The current conditions of the farm and livestock operations before Fall 2021 were inadequate access for students, faculty, and livestock simultaneously, inadequate access for student learning because of safety and space, inadequate space for research, inadequate space causing undue stress on animals during on and offloading, and inadequate space that requires the removal of the animals for lab classes away from their current location on a daily bases. ("Large Animal Building," n.d.).

Jacob Mayer, a Project Engineer and Northeast Agriculture Advisory Committee Member, stated, "good stockmanship is not learned in a textbook. It is developed over time with practice. Providing a facility that will allow opportunities for students to foster those skills is critically important" (J. Mayer, personal communication, June 2, 2021).

After phase one, the updates will include improved adequate facilities and modern high-tech equipment for a safer environment for students, faculty, and livestock, increased hands-on learning opportunities, reduction of the need to remove the animals from the facilities so frequently, and increased opportunities for research ("Large Animal Building," n.d.).

The Veterinary Technology Facility

The current conditions of the veterinary technology facility before Fall 2021 were inadequate space, lighting, and ceiling height, insufficient reception space, inconveniently located classrooms, lack of an on-site lab, and separated veterinary technology classes and laboratories over several buildings ("Veterinary Technology," n.d.).

Dr. Michael Cooper, D.V.M., Instructor and Director of the Veterinary Technology Program, stated:

> To meet the workforce need within the state, we are going to have to grow our enrollments. The equipment in the Northeast Veterinary Technology program is state of the art, but our building is outdated, undersized and inefficient. The laboratory and treatment areas, radiology and surgery, need to be larger to accommodate learning and be closer together to better mimic a typical working clinic and create efficiencies. ("Veterinary Technology," n.d., para. 4)

Updates in Phase One

The Phase 1 updates will include improved program courses, improved access to modern high-tech equipment, increased student enrollment, opportunities for better community outreach, and a facility with all the available Veterinary Technology Program resources ("Veterinary Technology," n.d.). The Veterinary Technology Program will change locations in Fall 2021 to the new Veterinary Technology Building located in phase one in the Agriculture and Water Center of Excellence. The Veterinary Technology Program at Northeast Community College is one of only two in the state of Nebraska (T. Kruse, personal communication, June 02, 2021).

Precision and Mechanized Agriculture

The conditions of precision and mechanized agriculture before Fall 2021 were inadequate space for larger equipment hands-on training, inadequate space for long-term large equipment projects without the repetition of setting up and removal, and inadequate safety during the hands-on learning ("Precision Agriculture," n.d.).

Steve Anderson, with Anderson and Anderson Insurance and a member of Northeast Board of Governors, stated:

> Northeast has a large farming operation that is very unique. Students need experience with planting technology, irrigation, combine monitors, and more. The Agriculture and Water Center of Excellence is going to prepare students for all of the new technologies that are coming. ("Precision Agriculture," n.d., para. 8)

After phase one, the updates will include modern lighting and proper safety features with adequate space, space for long-term large equipment projects without the repetition of setting up and removal, and hands-on learning in climate-controlled facilities ("Precision Agriculture," n.d.).

PHASE TWO

Phase two will consist of agriculture classrooms, agriculture complex expansion, greenhouse, innovation and demonstration center, and programmatic support. However, for the completion and visualization of phase two, the Northeast Community College Agriculture and Water Center of Excellence needs additional public and private support. The funding will determine the rate at which phase two will start and exactly which ideas will come to fruition ("Phase II," n.d.).

Agricultural Classrooms

The current conditions of the agriculture classrooms are too small for the current enrollment of Northeast Community College students, separate throughout the campus, and overcrowded with inadequate lab equipment storage. After phase two, the updates will include a new building devoted to classrooms and labs for the increased enrollment due to the popularity of the Agriculture, Food, and Natural Resources Programs at Northeast Community College. This new classroom addition will be located next to the additions in phase one ("Agriculture Classrooms," n.d.).

The current conditions of the agriculture complex expansion are inadequate arena space for hands-on learning and event gatherings, such as state and national agricultural shows, and inadequate infrastructure to host the larger agricultural shows. After phase two, the updates will include expanding the arena to meet current regulatory requirements and increasing the infrastructure for the larger agricultural shows ("Chuck M. Pohlman Agriculture Complex Expansion," n.d.).

Greenhouse Facility

The current conditions of the greenhouse are that it is too small to give the students advanced technology, has inadequate in climate control and is used by the college for the groundskeeping, thus decreasing the amount of space for student learning.

Kathy Goodwater, Horticulture Instructor, stated:

> So much new technology has been created in the horticulture arena that our present greenhouse is totally inadequate. Any student wanting to be competitive in today's job market in horticulture needs hands-on experience with plant irrigation systems, alarm monitors, venting systems, LED lighting, and hydroponics/aquaponics. (K. Goodwater, personal communication, June 2, 2021)

After phase two, the updates will include a massive greenhouse with classrooms, updated advanced technology, proper climate control, and proper hands-on learning.

The Agricultural Complex

The current conditions of the Chuck M. Pohlman Agriculture Complex are inadequate space for agriculture events, minimal community educational resources, and do not provide the ability to capitalize on visitors.

After phase two, the updates will include a larger lobby, updated interactive learning for the community, improved external stakeholder relationships, and a highlight of the next-generation agriculture technologies ("Innovation and Demonstration Center," n.d.).

In order to fulfill the requirements for instruction in the Center, more faculty will be required to provide the information on new and updated technologies and the new faculty will integrate the new applied research skills in the classroom. After phase two, the Northeast Community Center of Excellence will have evidence-based hands-on learning opportunities built around problem-solving with critical thinking ("Programmatic Support," n.d.).

FUNDING

The funding of the Northeast Community College Agriculture and Water Center of Excellence is a significant undertaking. For the first phase of the Northeast Community College Agriculture and Water Center of Excellence, approximately $22 million is needed. However, the total amount needed to complete phase one and phase two of the Northeast Community College Agriculture and Water Center of Excellence is approximately $80 million.

The Center of Excellence has already raised approximately $10 million from the college's local property taxes and approximately $12 million from private donations to the Northeast Community College Agriculture and Water Center of Excellence. These significant donations took about six years to raise from alumni, faculty, staff, community individuals, and businesses (T. Kruse, personal communication, June 02, 2021)

The Nexus Campaign

The Nexus means Nebraska is the intersection of the United States of America in agriculture technologies and is the heart of success and innovation to feed the world. In addition, the Nexus is more than a funding campaign for the Northeast Community College Agriculture and Water Center of Excellence.

The Nexus is the center of innovation and applied research for all areas of agriculture, giving Northeast Community College students hands-on learning applicable in agriculture worldwide. Lastly, the Nexus is the partnership between the Northeast Community College and the students, the communities, businesses, farmers, producers, and manufacturers the world over ("The Nexus Capital Campaign," n.d.).

STRENGTHS AND IMPROVEMENTS

To begin with, the Northeast Community College Agriculture and Water Center of Excellence is a future thinking and learning project. The Northeast Community College Agriculture and Water Center of Excellence is anticipating the agriculture issues in advance of thirty years and has begun preparing for those impacts. The Northeast Community College Agriculture and Water Center of Excellence is concerned with the 2050 food crisis because of the increase in the world population, and the impact the increase will have on water and agriculture productions, with an estimated increase of over fifty percent for agriculture productions.

Further, the Northeast Center of Excellence is concerned about the recent unstable weather patterns, and temperature increases the world has been facing. The number of people worldwide, including the United States, lacking food and living with food insecurities is also a concern. Therefore, the Northeast Community College Agriculture and Water Center of Excellence stands as the Nexus to help resolve these problems through innovation and applied research in all areas of agriculture ("The 2050 Food Crisis," n.d.).

In addition, was the wealth of information about the Agriculture and Water Center of Excellence located on the internet? This website covered the vision, the plan, the Nexus, and the engagement of the Northeast Community College Agriculture and Water Center of Excellence ("Agriculture and Water Center of Excellence," n.d.).

However, Dr. Kruse noted that the Northeast Community College Agriculture and Water Center of Excellence website was not a significant source of fundraising. The fundraising came from the hard work of many folks speaking with, calling, and meeting folks to discuss the Northeast Community College Agriculture and Water Center of Excellence (T. Kruse, personal communication, June 02, 2021).

One weakness noted by Dr. Kruse is that the Northeast Community College Agriculture and Water Center of Excellence did not partner earlier with universities or other colleges. Connecting sooner with these important partnerships could have made fundraising easier for the Northeast Community College Agriculture and Water Center of Excellence (T. Kruse, personal communication, June 02, 2021).

CONCLUSION

The Northeast Community College Agriculture and Water Center of Excellence is an excellent opportunity for the students of Northeast Community College. The positive impacts of the Northeast Community College Agriculture and Water Center of Excellence will be felt by the communities, businesses, farmers, producers, manufacturers, and consumers the world over because of the innovation and applied research in all areas of agriculture.

REFERENCES

Agriculture Classrooms | Nexus Campaign - Northeast Community College. (n.d.). Retrieved June 23, 2021, from Nexus website: https://agwaternexus.com/agriculture-classes/

Agriculture & Water Center of Excellence | Northeast Community College. (n.d.). Retrieved from Nexus website: https://agwaternexus.com/

Chuck M. Pohlman Agriculture Complex Expansion | Nexus Campaign. (n.d.). Retrieved June 25, 2021, from Nexus website: https://agwaternexus.com/agriculture-complex-expansion/

College Farm & Livestock | Nexus - Northeast Community College. (n.d.). Retrieved June 22, 2021, from Nexus website: https://agwaternexus.com/farm-livestock-operations/

College, N. C. (n.d.). Agriculture, Food, and Natural Resources | Career Field | Academics. Retrieved June 3, 2021, from Northeast Community College website: https://northeast.edu/academics/career-fields/19-agriculture-food-and-natural-resources

College, N. C. (September 15, 2016). New Northeast center will work to improve soil health and water conservation | News. Retrieved June 3, 2021,

Center of Excellence for Agriculture and Water   69

from Northeast Community College website: https://northeast.edu/news/article/2077-new-northeast-center-will-work-to-improve-soil-health-and-water-conservation

College, N. C. (December 17, 2019a). Coordinating commission approves new agriculture facilities at Northeast | News. Retrieved June 3, 2021, from Northeast Community College website: https://northeast.edu/news/article/3447-coordinating-commission-approves-new-agriculture-facilities-at-northeast

College, N. C. (December 28, 2019b). Northeast's ag programs serve critical need in training a future workforce | News. Retrieved June 3, 2021, from Northeast Community College website: https://northeast.edu/news/article/3450-northeasts-ag-programs-serve-critical-need-in-training-a-future-workforce

Innovation & Demonstration Center | Northeast Community College. (n.d.). Retrieved June 25, 2021, from Nexus website: https://agwaternexus.com/innovation-demonstration/

Large Animal Building | Nexus - Northeast Community College. (n.d.). Retrieved June 23, 2021, from Nexus website: https://agwaternexus.com/large-animal-handling/

Phase I - Spring 2020. (n.d.). Retrieved June 22, 2021, from Nexus website: https://agwaternexus.com/phase-i-spring-2020/

Phase II - Future Growth. (n.d.). Retrieved June 22, 2021, from Nexus website: https://agwaternexus.com/phase-ii-future-growth/

Precision Agriculture | Mechanized Agriculture | Nexus Capital Campaign. (n.d.). Retrieved June 23, 2021, from Nexus website: https://agwaternexus.com/precision-mechanized-agriculture/

Programmatic Support | Nexus Campaign - Northeast Community College. (n.d.). Retrieved June 25, 2021, from Nexus website: https://agwaternexus.com/programmatic-support/

The 2050 Food Crisis | Nexus Campaign for Sustainable Agriculture. (n.d.). Retrieved June 25, 2021, from Nexus website: https://agwaternexus.com/2050-food-crisis/

The Nexus Capital Campaign | Agriculture & Water Center of Excellence. (n.d.). Retrieved June 1, 2021, from Nexus website: https://agwaternexus.com/the-nexus/

Veterinary Technology | Nexus Capital Campaign for Nebraska Agriculture. (n.d.). Retrieved June 23, 2021, from Nexus website: https://agwaternexus.com/vet-tech/

Chapter 7

Center of Excellence for International Studies

Timothy Gwillim

Founded in 1682, Philadelphia, Pennsylvania has always played an important part in the history and culture of the United States. It quickly became one of the leading cities in the founding of the United States and served as the country's capital city for a time. The city quickly grew and became one of the largest in the nation, welcoming many immigrant groups. Today the city remains one of the important cities in the United States with a thriving diverse population.

Located in Philadelphia, the Community College of Philadelphia works to teach students how to exhibit the moniker, the City of Brotherly Love, of the city. Philadelphia is a diverse major city in which many people of different nationalities and ethnicities reside. The Community College of Philadelphia believes its mission is to teach students to become informed citizens in the culturally diverse city.

The college works to accomplish this mission in several different ways including hosting the Center for International Understanding, (CIU). The CIU strives to teach students intercultural competence so that they will be better informed as they graduate and enter society.

COMMUNITY COLLEGE OF PHILADELPHIA

Benjamin Franklin, one of Philadelphia's famous early residents, believed in education. He was instrumental in forming the country's first subscription library and the University of Pennsylvania. Even though these were founded during Franklin's lifetime, Philadelphia would not have a public institution of higher education until the Community College of Philadelphia was founded in 1964 (Community College of Philadelphia website, n.d.).

The college opened its doors to students in 1965 in a former department store building. The college would then acquire a former Philadelphia Mint building in 1971 and begin holding classes there in 1973. The college maintained both locations for a while until moving all instruction to the location of the former mint building. Today the college has continued in this location and has a 14-acre urban campus.

The college enrolls approximately 25,000 credit and noncredit students of which 12,000 are full-time students. The college offers more than 100 associate degree, academic and proficiency certificate programs (Community College of Philadelphia website, n.d.).

The college enrolls a diverse student population. African-American students are the largest population at the college with 41% of the student body. The college also enrolls 23% White, 16% Hispanic/Latino, 11% Asian/Pacific Islander, 4% Other/Unknown, 3% students of two or more races, and 2% Non-resident alien. The percentage numbers show the fact that 72% of the student population is made up of minority students.

Mission of CCP

The Community College of Philadelphia strives to educate students to become part of the world in which they find themselves. The college mission statement says that the college "serves Philadelphia by preparing it students to be informed and concerned citizens, active participants in the cultural life of the city, and enable to meet the changing needs of business, industry, and the professions" (Community College of Philadelphia website, n.d.).

The college also states that a part of the mission is to educate students to have an increased "awareness and appreciation of a diverse world where all are interdependent" (Community College of Philadelphia website, n.d.). The college also strives to develop and prepare the students to be global citizens.

The Need for Global Citizens

With this backdrop, the college became an early adopter of international education among community colleges. Wanting to fulfill their mission of preparing students to be global citizens, the college decided to enroll international students in 1997. The international students who enrolled found themselves in classes with students from other countries. The students gained access to internationalization by just attending classes with the international students.

The college also began offering short term study abroad in 2000. The first program offered allowed students to study English literature in London. A few years later a second program was added that allowed students to study Spanish and Sociology in Costa Rica. Since that time, the college has continued to offer short term study abroad offerings for students. Although the study abroad programs were few in the beginning, the impact that they had, along with the international students who arrived on campus, was profound for students and faculty alike.

INTERNATIONAL CONTENT INTO THE CURRICULUM

The college did not stop with just offering study abroad and welcoming international students to the campus. The college also had some faculty who pushed for internationalization of the college curriculum. These faculty put international content into their own classes and then encouraged other faculty to do the same. Putting international content into the general curriculum gave students a different perspective not only about the city of Philadelphia, but also about the world outside of the city.

The push from the few members of the faculty that were concerned was heard on campus. Soon work was beginning on the task. In order to help and encourage the work, grant proposals were submitted. Two Title VI grants were obtained to expand the curriculum to introduce the study of non-Western cultures (Fragouli, 2020).

Leadership

One of the key proponents in this project was David Prejsnar. Prejsnar had been at the college for over a decade at that time. He constantly worked to secure grants and to encourage faculty to put international content in the courses. He also worked to get students into the courses and encourage the study abroad opportunities. Prejsnar's education was grounded in Japanese Buddhism. He used this background to create a new course for the college. The course studied Japanese culture and civilization.

Other faculty began creating courses during this time to introduce more international flavor to the course offerings. Courses were added that highlighted African cultures and civilizations and a humanities course about cultural traditions. These courses broadened the course selections for students while at the same time teaching the students about international cultures.

PROGRAM IN INTERNATIONAL STUDIES

Not only were new courses added to the catalog, but the college added a new program of offering, International Studies. The International Studies program was developed to cultivate leaders who have a global mindset. The program teaches students global perspectives on various world cultures, intercultural understanding and communication, and critical thinking skills with an international filter (Community College of Philadelphia website, n.d.).

The international studies program allows students to focus on various areas of the world while taking their general education classes. The students are required to attend several of the international festivals that the college sponsors. They also have time to interact with students from various international cultures throughout the program.

While enrolled in the program the students complete their general education requirements. New courses were developed for the program such as Introduction to Global Studies. Students are also required to take International Relations courses as well several world history and civilization courses. Another requirement for the students is that they must take a single foreign language through the intermediate level. A course in intercultural communication is also required (Community College of Philadelphia website, n.d.).

Program Goal

The goal of the program is designed to allow a student to transfer to a four-year major in a like field. The program is designed under the Associate of Arts umbrella so that students will be able to transfer easily. The college has well established transfer agreements in place that allow the student to finish their bachelor's degree without any trepidation.

AWARD FOR OVERALL CAMPUS INTERNATIONALIZATION

Because of the work that the college had completed toward the internationalization of the campus, attention to their work was recognized. Starting in 2003 and every year thereafter, the National Association for Foreign Student Affairs (NAFSA) awards higher educational institutions an award for overall campus internationalization. Since 2007, this award has been known as the Senator Paul Simon Award for Comprehensive Internationalization and is awarded annually to high achievers in the field.

The award was established in 2003, and the Community College of Philadelphia was among the year's award winners. The college received the award due to the work that had been completed to provide international content to the students. Much work had been put into creating the international content, creating new classes with the international focus, and submitting and receiving grants to support this work.

DEVELOPING THE CENTER FOR INTERNATIONAL UNDERSTANDING

After receiving the accolades for being an early adopter among community colleges of internationalizing the college, the Community College of Philadelphia began considering the best method of pulling these efforts together. The college did not want to just rest on their laurels from the NAFSA award, but wanted to continue to develop and internationalize the campus. After much contemplation, a decision was made to consolidate the efforts into one place.

The Center for International Understanding at the Community College of Philadelphia was developed and started in 2009. Its overall purpose was to be a central point of international education at the college. It was the place in which study abroad programs, the International Studies major, a home for the international students, and the internationalization of the curriculum would reside. It also would become the central point for grant writing for the international development of the college.

With the development of the center, a purpose and mission statement for the center needed to be developed. A mission statement for the center was developed and posted on the college website.

The mission statement of the center reads:

> Community College of Philadelphia's Center for International Understanding promotes knowledge and appreciation of a diverse and interdependent world. The Center encourages and supports the integration of international content into courses and curricula, as well as student and faculty experiential learning abroad. To foster student achievement and enrichment, the Center supports faculty development and research. Drawing upon rich resources within the College and among outside organizations, businesses and individuals, the Center initiates and sustains projects to benefit the entire College community and to serve local, national and international needs. (Community College of Philadelphia website, n.d.).

College Mission

The mission statement shows that the Community College of Philadelphia has a commitment to training their students to become global citizens. The statement highlights that one of the best ways to encourage international development of the curriculum is to encourage personal international growth of the faculty. Once the faculty have experienced an international study abroad experience, they are much more likely to incorporate these experiences and international content into their courses.

The international content in courses has an effect on students by encouraging them to study abroad in order to gain expanded experience. In this regard, once momentum has been generated among the faculty, then students begin to want more international content. When students look for more international content, then momentum among the student body grows and encourages more growth in international education at the college.

The mission statement also highlights the building of partnerships to encourage and fund international activities. The COE was designed to be the central point of grant writing for international development of the college. Much work at the Center was done to secure grants. The Center also worked to develop outside partners to fund and develop international education. Partnerships with local universities, museums, and international organizations were developed to provide financial support as well as providing opportunities for international activities.

The creation of the COE and the focus on international development of the college showed that the Community College of Philadelphia was willing to not just talk about the importance of international development, but put the work needed into developing international education at the college.

The college was willing to put effort and resources into international development of the college because the college realized the importance of developing their students to become international citizens. The mission of international development for the college and the students was not just something they put on the website to promote, but rather, something that the college very much believed had purpose for the students who enrolled in the college's programs.

OPERATION AND OUTCOMES OF THE CENTER

With the establishment of the COE in 2009, the college began a centralized effort to expand international education. The Center contained the study abroad programs as well as the International Studies Associate of Arts degree. Through the years, changes have been made according to the growth of these items (D. Prejsnar personal communication, May, 27, 2021).

Study Abroad Program

The study abroad program was moved out of the COE in 2015. A director of the study abroad program was created that year to direct the program separate of the Center. The goal was to allow the Center and the study abroad programs to grow at a more rapid pace with a director for each program (D. Prejsnar personal communication, May, 27, 2021).

Likewise, the International Studies Associate of Arts degree was moved out of the Center around the same time as the study abroad program. The degree was moved out of the jurisdiction of the Center in order for the degree and the Center to grow. The degree was moved to the Liberal Arts and Communications division of the college with the other Associate of Arts programs.

Focus of the Center

With the previously mentioned moves, the Center for International Understanding was tasked with three main tasks to expand the internationalization of the campus. The main task of the Center was to work with faculty so that they would be able to internationalize the content in their current courses.

The task entailed the Center encouraging faculty to include international content into their courses. The Center developed a standardized form for faculty to use that would help them imbed this content (D. Prejsnar personal communication, May 27, 2021). The Center would also work with faculty to create new courses that would focus on international topics.

The second outcome of the Center was to develop and run co-curricular activities for the college. These activities would be non-credit events and programming that would be open for all faculty, staff, and students to attend. These activities would come from a variety of sources including faculty which have a unique knowledge in an internationalize topic, departments of local universities, local museums and historical centers, and local residents from the city of Philadelphia. The Center works with all of these areas to develop an international activity schedule for each academic year and promote these activities among the college community.

Community Partnerships

The Center has placed an emphasis on community partnerships. The Center has been able to develop relationships with the University of Pennsylvania in which the two institutions have shared funding from a Title VI grant to promote activities. The Center has developed partnerships with the University of Pennsylvania's South Asia Center, East Asia Center, and Middle East Center for research.

The Center has developed a partnership with Presbyterian Historical Society in Philadelphia using the societies historical research about missionary work in foreign countries to study the cultures of the foreign countries. Finally, the Center has worked with Howard University's Africa Center for research and activities.

Grant Opportunities

The third outcome of the Center was to continuously be looking for grant opportunities to fund the Center. The funds from grants also help the Center when they are working with faculty in their curriculum development. The Center has been successful in securing grants to fund research and activities. The funding opportunities provided due to the university partnerships has helped in the budget of the Center (D. Prejsnar personal communication, May 27, 2021).

All of the above outcomes are done with only one employee. David Prejsnar became the director of the Center for International Understanding in March of 2021. He is a long-time member of the faculty at the college and has been active in the Center's activities during his time at the college. He serves as the director while still maintaining his faculty role at the college.

The Center also completes these activities without any budget support from the college. The funding that the Center secures is the sole method of supporting activities. The Center does not have a designated office to run the activities. The Center does serve as a way to pull together all of the activities, curriculum work, and funding for the internationalization of the college.

ANALYSIS OF THE OUTCOMES

The Community College of Philadelphia was an early adopter among community colleges in internationalization of the campus. Its early work in this area brought recognition to the college. The creation of the Center for International Understanding became the focus point of campus internationalization. Since the creation of the Center, the directors of the Center have worked to keep growing the amount of international content that students receive either through the content in curriculum or from college promoted activities.

Studies about campus internationalization have proven that the work has a positive effect on students understanding the world in which they live in (Fragouli, 2020; Gann, 2016; Walenkamp, 2020). The work that the Community College of Philadelphia and the Center for International Understanding has done has had a positive effect among the students over the years. Students of the college have been and will continue to be more ready to be global citizens because of the campus internationalization.

CONCLUSION

Campus internationalization is increasingly becoming an important part of a student's education. Community colleges should work to educate their students about the happenings and culture of the world. It is important the students understand both the history and culture of the country in which they live and other countries. With the rapid globalization of the world, students need to understand other cultures in order to become effective citizens and businesspeople.

The Community College of Philadelphia was an early adopter of internationalization and the college has continued the work through the years. It serves as an example for community colleges to look to when considering internationalizing their campus. The college has shown that through hard work and concerted effort campus internationalization can be achieved. The Center for International Understanding has played a large part in achieving this goal.

REFERENCES

Community College of Philadelphia website. (n.d.). https://www.ccp.edu.

Fragouli, E. (2020). Internationalizing the Curriculum. *International Journal of Higher Education Management.* 6(2), 18–30.

Gann, R. (2016). Introduction: Internationalizing the Curriculum—Reflections on Process, Design, and Delivery. *European Political Science,* 15(1), 1–6.

Walenkamp, J. (2020). Internationalizing the Curricula: The Motives. *Socialni Pedagogika,* 8(1).

Chapter 8

Center of Excellence for Learning Sciences

Shawn Guy

Tennessee State University (TSU) is a public, four-year institution located in Nashville. TSU can trace its roots back to 1909, when the Tennessee General Assembly created the Agricultural and Industrial Normal School, which would grow to become TSU. On June 19, 1912, the first group of 247 students began their academic careers under the leadership of Mr. William Jasper. Students would work together daily to keep the institution functioning; everyday activities included clearing rocks, harvesting crops, and moving chairs from class to class.

In 1922 the Agricultural and Industrial Normal School began to offer bachelorette degrees as a four-year teacher's college. The present-day TSU exists as the result of the merger on July 1, 1979, of the former Tennessee State University and the University of Tennessee at Nashville (About TSU An HBCU Legacy, 2020).

TSU, Tennessee's only public historically black institution, is home to 5,875 undergraduate and 1,376 graduate students. The main campus is in a residential setting, just outside of downtown Nashville. The 500-acre campus has 65 buildings and sets along the Cumberland River. The Avon Williams campus is located near the center of Nashville's business and government district. TSU has the unique distinction of being Middle Tennessee's first Carnegie Doctoral / Research University.

TSU offers 38 undergraduate degrees through nine different colleges: Agriculture, Business, Education, Engineering, Health Sciences, Liberal Studies, Life and Physical Science, and Public Service (Tennessee State University, 2020). Some of the notable alumni who have attended TSU include Oprah Winfrey, former Olympian Wilma Rudolph, and Jesse Russell, the microchip inventor (About TSU An HBCU Legacy, 2020).

THE CENTER OF EXCELLENCE FOR LEARNING SCIENCES

Tennessee State University is also home to the Center of Excellence for Learning Sciences (COELS). Learning Sciences is an interdisciplinary/multidisciplinary field that draws on multiple theoretical perspectives and research paradigms to advance knowledge about human learning and development in formal and informal settings (COE-LS News and Publications, 2020).

Researchers from disciplines including education, psychology, computer science, and anthropology collaborate to develop new ideas and methodologies about learning. Parents, teachers, administrators, policymakers, and educational researchers benefit from the research produced by learning scientists as they create new learning environments and classrooms.

Mission of the Center

COELS was established by the Tennessee General Assembly and the Governor of Tennessee to expand research in public higher education and contribute to the overall economic and community development base of the state. Founded in 1984, COELS has since become a hub for statewide training and professional development for early childhood professionals in Tennessee (Academic and Professional Development Programs, 2020):

> The mission of the Center of Excellence for Learning Sciences is to design and conduct multidisciplinary research and demonstrations concerning practices, policies, and programs that promote the educational, social, physical, and psychological well-being of children and families; and to disseminate research and information to improve public policy and

the programmatic decisions of agencies, schools, institutions, and communities in Tennessee, the nation, and the global community. (Academic and Professional Development Programs, 2020)

The center gained prominence after researching the effects of small class size. The research study grew in size and scope and became widely known as the Student/Teacher Achievement Ratio (STAR) project. The research produced outcomes that would later become the standard for student-teacher ratios for elementary grades (Academic and Professional Development Programs, 2020).

Operations

COELS is home to several different programs, including Social Services Competency-Based Training (CBT), the Tennessee Early Childhood Training Alliance (TECTA), the Tennessee Early Childhood Training Alliance (TECTA), the Tennessee State Early Head Start-Child Care Partnership, and the Tennessee Comprehensive Area Resource Efforts (TN CAREs) Early Head Start program. COELS has a management team led by Dr. Kimberly Smith. Dr. Smith is a seasoned Early Childhood professional who is responsible for the overall operation of COELS, including its $16 million budget.

Research

The foundation of the Center of Excellence is the research conducted by the staff members, which aimed to address the needs and priorities of the community. The study conducted by COELS concentrates on different areas of education including, K-12 teaching, adult learning, and higher education persistence and retention efforts (Coleman, 2020). Outcomes generated from these studies are used to create policy discussions that enhance educational practices.

As noted earlier, the STAR project was one of the first studies conducted by COELS. This four-year study produced findings that led to improved early learning and cognitive studies (Tennessee Early Childhood Program Administrator Credential (TECPAC)). The study also revealed the effect of small class size on the achievement of minority children was significantly positive.

Recently, COELS has produced studies that address gender and pay inequities in the childcare fields and the Impact of COVID 19 on the Early Childhood Community. The survey regarding gender and pay disparities in the childcare fields revealed women in the categories of high school diplomas and baccalaureate degrees make more money than men.

On the other hand, men make slightly more hourly pay than women in the types of graduate/professional degrees, associate degrees, and some college coursework. The study regarding gender and pay inequities has generated discussions on interventions such as occupational segregation, education and training, job classifications and pay systems, awareness-raising, and transparency (Lynch & Brown, 2020).

Research on COVID 19

The study of Impact of COVID 19 on the Early Childhood Community examined the effects of COVID-19 on early childhood professionals, parents, and their children by covering a broad range of childcare groups within the state. Researchers discovered that financial hardships for families and businesses, emotional drain for everyone, and concern of loss of learning and social connections for children were everyday issues among studied participant.

It also revealed that parents gained an increased knowledge of technology, improved capacity for change and resiliency, and welcomed the opportunity of more time with family. The study of Impact of COVID 19 on the Early Childhood Community has triggered comments regarding the health and safety of childcare workers during the pandemic and the digital divide among the rural residents in Tennessee (Smith, 2021).

Social Services Competency-Based Training

The Social Service Competency-Based Training (CBT) program is a national training program developed by COELS. The CBT program is designed to improve the knowledge and skills of human services workers working as practitioners in social service agencies, childcare facilities, and head start programs (Academic and Professional Development Programs, 2020). Participants delve into a curriculum that is structured to align with the Head Start Relationship-Based Competencies.

Human services professionals receive training across 25 functional areas and 64 competency-based lessons. Topics discussed during the training include motivation, culturally competent communication, financial literacy, professional ethics, resilience, group work, trauma, social network mapping, reflective practice, empowerment, professional development, and documentation. The curriculum is divided into three key areas: Skills: Working with People; Attitudes: Motivation through the Use of Self, and Knowledge: Systems and Human Behavior (Coleman, 2020).

The CBT program is nationally recognized and implemented by several states throughout the United States, including Tennessee, Oregon, and Idaho. Participants receive 90 hours of classroom instruction, field mentor observations, and competency-based evaluation. Over the past two years, the SSCBT program has seen a total of 50 graduates, and eight students have renewed their credentials.

Students completing the SSCBT program can receive undergraduate college credit from TSU. Graduates leave the program able to work in various family support and community services settings and address the priority areas outlined in the Head Start Family Worker Training Initiative (Coleman, 2020).

TENNESSEE EARLY CHILDHOOD TRAINING ALLIANCE

The Tennessee Early Childhood Training Alliance (TECTA) is a statewide program that provides training and academic tuition to childcare providers and administrators. TECTA began more than 25 years ago to address barriers to postsecondary educational attainment through quality professional development opportunities for Tennessee's early childhood workforce. Numerous studies had shown that teacher education and training were significant predictors of the quality of early childhood programs. Once a community-based project, TECTA has blossomed into a statewide training program for early childhood professionals (Coleman, 2020).

Focus on Five Areas

TECTA offers a free 30-hour orientation with instruction across five areas: center-based child care, infant/toddler child care, family child care, school-age child care, and administrator training. Participants who complete the orientation are eligible to receive tuition assistance. The funding provided by the TECTA program helps Tennessee childcare workers pursue postsecondary education opportunities while limiting the financial burden.

Traditionally, affordability has been a barrier for childcare workers who wish to further their education, as wages are below the national average. In 2020, the TECTA program provided over $1.1 million in tuition support for 825 students taking 2,132 courses. The TECTA also assisted 138 students with obtaining their Child Development Associate (CDA) Credential (Coleman, 2020).

TECTA Locations

There are eight different TECTA sites: Austin Peay State University, Chattanooga State Community College, Dyersburg State Community College, East Tennessee State University, Roane State Community College, Southwest Tennessee State Community College, Tennessee Tech University, and Tennessee State University. These sites are strategically located throughout the state in higher education institutions; that work to reach all early childhood programs and potential early childhood professionals across their service area.

Each of the TECTA sites serves as a local center that provides credentials, certificates, and degree training programs across all 95 counties in Tennessee. Each TECTA site hosts the 30-hour orientation class for its residents and serves as a resource for technical support and program accreditation (Coleman, 2020).

Child Development Associate

The Child Development Associate (CDA) Training Program is a national credentialing initiative supported by the National Association for the Education of Young Children (NAEYC). The CDA Credential is awarded by the Council for Professional Recognition and is widely recognized among early childhood professionals. The NAEYC standards and competencies build upon the information that is taught during the TECTA orientation.

The focus of the CDA Training Program is to help early childhood professionals improve the quality of performance of individual staff members in their role as child caregivers (Coleman, 2020). During the 2019–2020 academic year, TECTA sites provided scholarship funding for 1,044 CDA Prep courses, and a total of 86 earned or were in the process of reaching the credential (Alliance, 2020).

The Early Childhood Program Administrator Credential

The Tennessee Early Childhood Program Administrator Credential (TECPAC) is awarded to early childcare administrators and directors (Coleman, 2020). This 10-month program is delivered in a hybrid format providing candidates the opportunity to interact online and face-to-face. Candidates are selected for the program based on their work experience and educational background.

TECPAC awardees receive the credentials, demonstrated specific competencies for effective leadership and management through academics, experience, and a portfolio assessment. TECPAC is recognized by the Tennessee Department of Human Services, which acknowledges the well-documented relationship between overall administrative practices and quality outcomes for children and families [Tennessee Early Childhood Program Administrator Credential (TECPAC)].

TENNESSEE STATE UNIVERSITY EARLY HEAD START-CHILD CARE PARTNERSHIP

TSUs Early Head Start partnership is a collaboration with private childcare providers. With oversight from COELS, private childcare facilities receive comprehensive child development and family support to 80 children in 10 classrooms via high-quality full-year, full-day services for qualified working families. The Tennessee Cares Early Head Start focuses on prevention and early intervention with low-income families.

COELS provides coordinated, comprehensive, intensive, and continuous support services to enable families to attain self-sufficiency while recognizing these families and children's integrity and unique needs.

Tennessee CAREs services Gibson, Henry, and Weakley counties in Northwest Tennessee and is federally funded to serve an enrollment of 112 children (Partnerships, 2020).

Strengths and Improvements

The COELS is an excellent example of how academics, research, and service can intersect to produce positive outcomes. The center has leveraged its veteran staff members to increase grant funding. The program benefits from dedicated professionals with rich experience and knowledge in early childhood education, research, training, and instruction. Staff members have a variety of experience that adds to the depth of knowledge at the center.

COELS has received positive reviews and increased grant funding over the past three years (K. Smith, personal touch, May 20, 2021). Last year alone, the TECTA program received a 22 percent increase in funding. The COELS has also received $50,000 to create online resources to help early childhood educators with college and career success. The center was awarded an additional $1 million to expand its Early Head Start Program (Brown, 2020).

The success of the COELS has caused minor issues related to resource allocations and program efficiencies. The scope of services offered through the COELS has increased; unfortunately, this requires additional resources, as both time and personnel are limited. Also, program activities are scheduled according to each program's funding cycle and scope of services, making cross-cutting research projects more difficult.

Students

Many students can benefit from programs offered through the COELS work in areas that deal with early childcare or human services. Any childcare worker working at a licensed facility can take courses at any TECTA sites located throughout the state. The initial orientation course is free. This is the only profitable program offered by the COELS. Human Services professionals can earn credentials that are provided through the COELS. The SSCBT Program attracts students from across the country.

Value

Although COELS received more than $16 million in funding last year, its value appears immeasurable. The center is responsible for nearly one-fifth of the total grant funding awarded to TSU. The COELS landed the university's largest grant total; $11.4 million. COELS also provides opportunities for low-wage childcare to gain additional training and education.

Students can complete the TECTA orientation program free of charge. Individuals who have completed the TECTA orientation program can receive tuition assistance to pursue advanced degrees. COELS also performs research and offers professional development that ultimately benefits childcare workers and their students.

Future

The future of COELS will continue to be centered around the needs of the community. The onset of the COVID 19 pandemic proved that the center must be adaptable, as the community's needs can change. The success of COELS will depend upon its ability to shift to meet the needs of the community in a timely and efficient manner. The COVID 19 pandemic also allowed COELS to infuse technology into their learning disciplines by offering online and hybrid courses.

Site visits were also conducted using web-based video conferencing software. The use of technology will continue to be a growing trend, as families and staff members have grown accustomed to these technological efficiencies. Lastly, research projects will continue to grow in size and scope. The Director of the COELS has prioritized research to gain additional funding for future programs and bolstering TSU's reputation among peer institutions.

CONCLUSION

COELS has been around for 25 years, dissecting ways to improve learning for our most vulnerable populations. The center uses a model that overlaps research, service, and academics. The study has proven to be a valuable source of revenue at TSU. Still, it has also enriched the lives of early childcare workers and their students by producing best practices and dialog around important issues.

The service component is remarkable, as the center provides training, tuition assistance, and recognition free of charge. Any licensed childcare worker in Tennessee can take advantage of these opportunities. COELS offers opportunities for early childhood professionals to a wide range of credentials, including certificates up to PhD. COELS functions at a high level, producing results that garnered recognition from across the United States.

REFERENCES

About TSU An HBCU Legacy. (July 20, 2020). Retrieved from Tennessee State University: https://www.tnstate.edu/about_tsu/history.aspx

Academic and Professional Development Programs. (July 20, 2020). Retrieved from Tennessee State University: https://www.tnstate.edu/learningsciences/about.aspx

Alliance, T. E. (2020). *TECTA Program Overview*. Nashville: Tennessee State University.

Brown, C. (2020). *Tennessee State University Center of Excellence Annual Report*. Nashville: Tennessee State University Center of Excellence for Learning Sciences.

COE-LS News and Publications. (July 19, 2020). Retrieved from Tennessee State University: https://www.tnstate.edu/learningsciences/news-pubs.aspx

Coleman, K. (2020). Tennessee Early Childhood Training Alliance: Breaching, Reaching, and Teaching. *Journal of Community Engagement and Scholarship*, 1–5.

Lynch, D. E., & Brown, D. (2020). *Gender and Pay Inequity in the Child Care Field*. Nashville: Tennessee State University.

Partnerships, S. P. (July 17, 2020). Retrieved from Tennessee State University: https://www.tnstate.edu/learningsciences/service.aspx

Smith, D. K. (2021). *The Impact of COVD 19 on the Early Childhood Community*. Nashville: Tennessee State University.

Tennessee Early Childhood Program Administrator Credential (TECPAC). (n.d.).

Tennessee State University. (July 18, 2020). Retrieved from US News and World Report: https://www.usnews.com/best-colleges/tennessee-state-3522

Chapter 9

Center of Excellence for Manufacturing Innovation

Mark T. Rooze

How one measures industrial activity varies, but the Greenville-Spartanburg metroplex in South Carolina almost always makes it onto the list of America's top ten industrial areas. That development took root when Michelin North America, attracted by the area's history with textiles, opened its first plant in Greenville on March 10, 1975, with many more plants in the across the state to follow. In a few decades, the area became a center for automotive manufacturing, when in 1994 the first BMW rolled off the line at the Spartanburg assembly plant.

A TOTAL CONCEPT OF INDUSTRIAL EDUCATION

Today, a major contributor to the South Carolina's upstate industrial activity is the Gene Haas Center for Manufacturing Innovation (CMI) of Greenville Technical College at the Clemson University International Center for Automotive Research CU-ICAR, located just off I-85. CMI shares the greenspace-laden Millennium Campus with the CU-ICAR and Greenville School District's Dr. Phinnize J. Fisher Middle School. However, the educational contribution to the transition of Upstate industry from textile-based to automotive and heavy-industrial-based nearly imploded when educators' dreams did not match those of area industrial leaders.

The Growth of the Millennium Campus

In the early 2000s, plans for building Clemson University officials' dream project, the Clemson University Center for Motor Sports Excellence, were well underway. Central to the project was a $50 million wind tunnel built for research modeled after facilities in Europe. Many resources were already committed.

As John Warner (2020) tells the story, Clemson Vice President of Research Chris Przirembel approached BMW Manufacturing's president, Helmut Leube, with the plan for BMW to rent time on the wind tunnel. A few minutes into the presentation, Helmut said, "We don't need research here." Given the effort put into developing the plan, Chris kept going. Helmut again said, "We don't need research," yet Chris continued. The third time Helmut said, "Chris, BMW has research in Germany and doesn't need research in South Carolina," Chris closed his laptop, crestfallen.

Then Chris asked the only question remaining. What was BMW's problem that Clemson could solve? Helmut said BMW needed to attract and develop world-class talent. The seed sprouted that became the Clemson University International Center for Automotive Research, CU-ICAR. (Warner, 2020, n.p.)

Changing directions midstream from academic dreams to industrial realities was difficult, and lawsuits were even filed over the changes. But today, BMW's wisdom has borne fruit, and not only is CU-ICAR a model for educating industrial engineers, "the Greenville area now has more OEMs and first-tier suppliers than Detroit" (National Research Council, 2009, p. 88).

External Support

Another contributor to CMI development was Miami-based real estate investor and philanthropist Cliff Rosen, who handpicked the site for the Millennium Campus and purchased it through Hollingsworth Funds. Rosen donated $42 million in the form of bargain sales of land to Clemson University Foundation and CU-ICAR. He furthered his donations at the Millennium Campus with $4 million for the Dr. Phinnize J. Fisher Middle School and $4.4 million for Greenville Tech's Gene Haas Center for Manufacturing Innovation ("The History of CU-ICAR," 2015).

Greenville Technical College President Keith Miller said that the Center for Manufacturing Technology would not have been possible in this form without Rosen's contribution. "The location for our new CMI is an ideal location because of its proximity to Clemson University's ICAR," said Miller, who collaborated with Clemson University on the project. "Cliff [Rosen] helped make that happen" ("The History of CU-ICAR," 2015, n.p.).

NASCAR: Gene Haas Support

A third major contributor to making the Center for Manufacturing Innovation a reality is Gene Haas. Motorsports fans may associate his name with the Stewart-Haas Racing Team of NASCAR and IndyCar fame or the Haas Formula One team, but in the industry, Haas is known as the largest machine tool builder in the western world, manufacturing a complete line of CNC products at competitive prices with industry-leading specifications.

The Gene Haas Foundation began establishing partnerships with many colleges in 2014 to encourage CNC training and manufacturing education, and at the time of this writing had created 39 buildings and manufacturing labs worldwide (Gene Haas Foundation, n.d.). The Gene Haas Foundation provided CMI with scholarships and equipment totaling over $2 million, as well as perhaps even more valuable expertise.

There are many more pieces to the puzzle that make up Greenville Tech's Center for Manufacturing Innovation. The list of local industries and manufacturers that have somehow contributed includes such companies as "BMW, Michelin, GE, Bosch Rexroth, ADEX Machining Technologies, League Manufacturing, JTEKT Koyo, Fabri-Kal, SpecFab Services, Master PT, Standard Motor Products and more" ("Groundbreaking," 2015).

Collaboration with K-12

Another piece of the puzzle is the K-12 component through Greenville County Schools. The Dr. Phinnize J. Fisher Middle School shares a portion of the Millennium Campus with CU-ICAR and the CMI. This deep integration with the K-12 sector is part of the industrial education strategy for the CMI, with options for coursework starting in K-12 that will transition to GTC and then to Clemson.

> The center will engage K-12 students and show them the possibilities that exist in advanced manufacturing careers through dual enrollment programs, tours, camps, and open houses. The Center for Manufacturing Innovation will be designed, literally, to change negative perceptions about manufacturing, with architectural features that engage from the first moment. ("Groundbreaking," 2015)

The rest of the Greenville community was behind CMI as well, approving a $25 million bond issue to help build the facility.

Important People

One of the final components needed was a director for the Center with the engineering experience to make it all happen. Greenville Tech found its man in the person of Dr. Abul Hasan, Dean of the School of Advanced Manufacturing and Engineering Technology and Director of the Center for Manufacturing Innovation, who was appointed in March 2020. Hasan earned his bachelor's degree in electrical engineering at the University of Engineering and Technology in Bangladesh, a master's degree in electrical engineering at the University of North Dakota, and a Ph.D. in electrical engineering from the University of Wyoming (Putnam, 2020).

He was involved in industry as an assistant engineer for the Bangladesh Power Development Board and as an engineer with Tripoli Electricity Corporation in Libya. Hasan worked in higher education for 28 years with more than 12 years in leadership before coming to Greenville Tech. He served as dean of the School of Engineering Technologies at Oklahoma State University Institute of Technology, director of academic affairs for the Australian College of Kuwait, and academic dean for George Mason University's Ras Al Khaimah Campus in the United Arab Emirates (Putnam, 2020).

The other faculty are special as well. Dr. Hasan explains:

> When we hire faculty, we are not looking for a professional teacher. We are looking for professionals who work in industry and will become a teacher. A lot of Ph.Ds. do not have that much hands-on training. We hire someone who has been working in industry and probably has a bachelor's or master's degree. We hire them as an adjunct, and if they like it, we ask them if they would like to move in full time. So, they have probably 20 years of experience with the robots and all these things, and that's what we need to help our students (A. Hasan, personal communication, May 17, 2021).

For that reason, CMI maintains contact with all the industries in the area, such as GE and BMW, because they need to draw from all these places. Students also are drawn not only from K-12 schools but industry as well. Some workers find that, after a few years, they have run up against a glass ceiling that they could break through only with an associate degree. AMET and CMI are exactly what these workers need (A. Hasan, personal communication, May 17, 2021).

OPPORTUNITIES FOR STUDY

Greenville Tech lists the Center for Manufacturing Innovation (CMI) as a site, not a program. Most programs contained therein are part of Greenville Tech's School of Advanced Manufacturing and Engineering Technology (AMET).

A Bachelor's Degree at a Technical College

A unique offering among Greenville Tech's AMET programs is the Bachelor in Applied Science in Advanced Manufacturing Technology. First authorized in 2018, it is to date the only bachelor's degree offered in the South Carolina Technical College System ("Governor," 2018). Applicants must have completed an associate degree in Mechatronics, Machine Tool, CNC, or one of three Engineering Technology degrees. Up to 42 credit hours are transferred from the associate degree to the bachelor's program; students who lack the required credits may take additional electives ("School," 2021).

The Applied Baccalaureate in Advanced Manufacturing Technology at Greenville Technical College will not duplicate anything offered by a four-year institution and will be very different from a traditional bachelor's degree. The degree will be technical in focus with a project-based curriculum. Learning will be active, engaging, and hands-on. ("Governor," 2018)

Machine Tool and CNC Programs

In the areas of Computer Numeric Control (CNC) and Machine Tool Technology, the school offers both associate degrees and certificates. In Machine Tool Technology, students learn basic metal shaping with milling machines, lathes, and grinders, learn tool construction, and learn how to program CNC machines both manually and with CAD/CAM software. ("School," 2021).

The Computer Numeric Control program focuses on the automated control of these machine tools, using high-end software to produce the instructions that control 5-axis CNC mills, 4-axis CNC mills, mill/turn CNC lathes, and 4-axis wire electric discharge machining (EDM) ("School," 2021).

Students practice these skills in the high-bay manufacturing space at CMI. Although there are smaller manual lathes and milling machines for the early development of concepts and skills, the dominant machines in the space are the Haas machines, including a Haas ST20-Y CNC lathe spinning at 4000 rpm, and the massive 4-and 5-axis Haas machines, including the massive Haas UMC 750 that works at 8100 rpm. These are extremely powerful machines that some other industrial training centers reserve for production only, but Dr. Hasan says that CMI students operate these machines as part of their program (A. Hasan, personal communication, May 17, 2021).

Some of the Phillips machines that are on the floor primarily for demo purposes are also used for student training. This hands-on experience produces students that are ready for a high-production industrial workplace. In addition, Bosch Rexroth sponsors internships in Machine Tool Technology, getting students out of the lab and into the workplace (A. Hasan, personal communication, May 17, 2021).

For measuring tolerances on the parts they produce, Greenville Tech CMI students can train on Renishaw's industry-leading metrology equipment such as laser interferometers and telescoping ball-bars which are used in advanced manufacturing to ensure that parts conform to specifications. In December 2019, Greenville Tech and Renishaw signed an agreement establishing the CMI as Renishaw's Southeastern Training Center ("Greenville Technical College and Renishaw," 2019).

Mechanical, Electronic, and Mechatronic Technology Degrees and Certificates

The Center for Manufacturing Innovation offers associate degrees and certificates in Mechanical Engineering Technology. Machine and CAD design, project and materials management, manufacturing processes, and quality assurance are all part of the program ("School," 2021). As with the CNC program, CMI students get to work with top-flight inspection and testing equipment, as well as modern coordinate measurement machines. They also work in the robotics lab located in the high-bay manufacturing space at the north end of CMI.

More than a dozen two-to-three-foot-tall industrial robots form a student learning space in the center of the floor; several larger robotic arms occupy glassed-in spaces for larger projects. These are furnished by CMI partner Kuka Robotics, and some from Danish manufacturer Universal Robots and ABB Robotics are used as well. The hydraulics lab equipment is also used in the Mechanical Engineering associate degree program. The School of Advanced Manufacturing and Engineering Technology (AMET) offers a transfer track to a four-year engineering degree (A. Hasan, personal communication, May 17, 2021).

The CMI also houses facilities for AMET's Electronics Engineering Technology program. This program can lead to an associate degree with promising salaries. As with the Mechanical Engineering Technology program, a transfer track program is available. Students have found work at BMW, Michelin, Duke Power, Fluor, GE, Mitsubishi, other employers.

Another program offered at CMI is Mechatronics Technology. This program was formerly known as Industrial Maintenance Technology. But today's industrial factories are white-glove clean, which does not match the almost janitorial connotation of the word maintenance. So, Mechatronics was chosen as a more apt name for the first line repairman on an industrial floor. When something goes wrong, it may be something mechanical—a bolt has loosened—or electrical—a wire has shorted out. The quickest route to getting the manufacturing line up and running again is to have a technician with some training in all these areas.

Greenville Tech's Mechatronics degree offers students some training in electrical, electronics, hydraulics, pneumatics, computer control, robotics, and MIG welding. Solenoids, programmable logic controllers (PLCs), and mechanical elements are all in the mechatronics domain. Emphasis is on troubleshooting, equipment installation, and preventive and first-line maintenance (A. Hasan, personal communication, May 17, 2021).

Engineering Design Technology

More than a dozen two-to-three-foot-tall industrial robots form a student learning space in the center of the floor; several larger robotic arms occupy glassed-in spaces for larger projects. The major programs used are AutoCAD, SolidWorks, and Dassault's CATIA V5. 3D imaging using Virtual Reality and 3D printing are part of the program, as they are for the Architectural Engineering Technology and Construction Engineering Technology associate degrees.

Renishaw, Inc. was one of CMI's partners from the beginning, supplying equipment for advanced additive technologies, otherwise known as 3D printing. Greenville Tech's CMI was Renishaw's first collaboration in additive technology with education ("Greenville Technical College and Renishaw," 2019).

Architectural Engineering Technology and Construction Engineering Technology

CMI offers two associate degrees related to construction, one in Architectural Engineering Technology and one in Construction Engineering Technology. Each degree program also has a transfer track to four-year universities. The architectural degree focuses on the design element, how the components of building processes come together, and how to capture structural elements on drawings. It includes courses in materials, statics, and building codes. It also has a hefty component of CAD, 3D modeling, Virtual Reality, and 3D printing ("School," 2021).

The Construction Engineering Technology degree focuses more on the building aspect. Graduates are prepared to take the South Carolina General Contractors and Residential Contractors exams. The program requires one year of work experience under a licensed contractor. Like the architectural engineering technology degree, this program includes courses in materials, statics, building codes, CAD, and Virtual Reality for Building Information Modeling (BIM) ("School," 2021).

Building Information Modeling (BIM) is the next step in improving construction efficiency, and it proves that 3D Virtual Reality goggles are not just toys for gamers. Although the concept of a master builder has been around for centuries, until 1979 the American Institute of Architects' code of ethics prohibited architects from engaging in construction. This disjuncture between designer and builder often resulted in architects drawing designs that, almost like an M.C. Escher print, no builder could construct in the real world. In the 1980s this distinction was erased, and by 1993 the Design-Build Institute of America (DBIA) had formed.

The construction industry found that having the architect work in the same firm with the contractor facilitated constant communication, avoided costly mistakes and time overruns, and delivered a better building at a lower cost. Building Information Modeling (BIM) is the next step. The building can be constructed virtually in 3D, and every component from every system can be examined before building materials or construction time are ever committed.

As a result, the clash between a concrete girder and a plumbing pipe or HVAC conduit, for example, is detected before construction begins. The necessary bend is built into the pipe or conduit as it is installed, and there is less demolition of previous construction, resulting in fewer delays, and cost overruns. Indeed, the pipe or conduit may be assembled off-site to arrive according to just-in-time standards.

THE CENTER FOR MANUFACTURING INNOVATION AND INDUSTRIAL GROWTH

CMI offers the Greenville community a meeting space in the midst of the manufacturing hub. In fact, the space between the upper and lower floors is bridged not only by elevators and stairs but also by the Wells

Fargo Theater, and indoor amphitheater. Meeting in an industrial space makes industrial proposals seem more real to civic officials (A. Hasan, personal communication, May 17, 2021).

And the CMI also contains a small business incubator. If an individual wants to start a company but lacks money or resources, the CMI can rent out a small space for the business to come in and try to get started. Machines, students, and faculty are available to help. The hope is that these start-ups will succeed and build their business in the Greenville area. As of this writing, the CMI has six businesses occupying incubator space (A. Hasan, personal communication, May 17, 2021).

Collaborative Support

But these services are not limited to the CMI. As a unique collaboration between Greenville Technical College, Clemson University, manufacturing technology suppliers, and local industry, CMI's manufacturing capabilities are available to industry partners, start-up firms, and other manufacturers seeking to develop, prototype and manufacture new products ("Machine and metrology," n.d.).

With CU-ICAR located nearby, there are plenty of opportunities for interaction between the schools. ICAR actually has a space in the northeast corner of the CMI. Clemson students come over with a design for prototyping, and the Greenville CMI students have the skills to build the part they need. Clemson students will test the part and come back with any modifications needed. Greenville Tech students will then fabricate the new part. This shared ICAR space has evolved due to the symbiotic relationship between the schools (A. Hasan, personal communication, May 17, 2021).

CMI program enrollment has grown rapidly, with a 12.78percent enrollment increase in mechatronics, machine tool, and manufacturing-related continuing education programs in the fall of 2019 over fall 2018 ("Greenville Technical College and Renishaw," 2019).

CONCLUSION

Greenville Tech's Gene Haas Center for Manufacturing Technology is a model of collaboration, not only horizontally between education and industry, but also vertically in education ranging from middle school through PhD. programs. There is good reason that this model should be followed elsewhere.

REFERENCES

Gene Haas Foundation. (n.d.) "Gene Haas Centers." *Gene Haas Foundation.* Retrieved from https://ghaasfoundation.org/content/ghf/en/Gene-Haas-Foundation-centers.html

Governor signs bill allowing Greenville Technical College to offer new baccalaureate degree program. August 22, 2018). *Greenville Technical College.* Retrieved from https://www.gvltec.edu/news/2018/08/governor-signs-bill-for-GTC-baccalaureate-degree.html

Greenville Technical College and Renishaw, Inc. enter into a training program agreement, establishing the Center for Manufacturing Innovation as Renishaw's southeastern training center. (December 3, 2019). *Greenville Technical College.* Retrieved from https://www.gvltec.edu/news/2019/12/renishaw-and-gtc-sign-agreement.html

Groundbreaking for Center for Manufacturing Innovation. (January 26, 2015). *Greenville Technical College.* Retrieved from https://www.gvltec.edu/news/2015/01/groundbreaking-for-center-for-manufacturing-innovation.html

Machine and metrology manufacturing services. (n.d.) *Greenville Technical College Center for Manufacturing Innovation.* Retrieved from https://cmi-greenville.com/machineserv.html

National Research Council. (2009). *Understanding Research, Science and Technology Parks: Global Best Practices: Report of a Symposium.* Washington, DC: The National Academies Press. https://doi.org/10.17226/12546.

Putnam, J. (March 9, 2020). Hasan to lead Greenville Tech's School of Advanced Manufacturing and Engineering Technology. *Greenville Journal.* Retrieved from https://greenvillejournal.com/education/hasan-brief/

School of Advanced Manufacturing and Engineering Technology. (2021). *Greenville Technical College: Academic Catalog 2021–2022 Edition.* Retrieved from https://catalog.gvltec.edu/school-advanced-manufacturing-engineering-technology/

The history of CU-ICAR is intertwined with story of Cliff Rosen. (January 29, 2015). *Upstate Business Journal.* Retrieved from https://upstatebusinessjournal.com/economic-development/history-cu-icar-intertwined-story-cliff-rosen/

Warner, J. (November 25, 2020). Be inspired by the amazing story the startup of a premier graduate engineering school. *Control your Destiny.* Retrieved from https://medium.com/control-your-destiny/seeing-opportunity-around-the-corner-how-a-startup-graduate-engineering-school-came-out-of-the-9f0d5b3d7e87

Chapter 10

Center of Excellence for Pharmacy

Candice Geiger

The Kennedy Pharmacy Innovation Center is an educational entity located in Columbia, South Carolina. This chapter explores the background, description and purpose, center operations, faculty, staff, and students, center outcomes, strengths and suggested improvements, value for students and service area, and the center's future.

BACKGROUND

The Kennedy Pharmacy Innovation Center is located within the University of South Carolina (USC) College of Pharmacy in Columbia, South Carolina. It was opened in 2010 with a generous gift from USC graduates Bill and Lou Kennedy. Bill Kennedy was a Pharmacy graduate from 1966, and Lou Kennedy was a Journalism graduate from 1984. The Kennedys donated $30 million with the intent to transform pharmacy education in conjunction with the USC College of Pharmacy (Gamecock Pharmacist, 2018).

The mission of the Center is to "be a catalyst that partners with faculty and students to revolutionize pharmacy education at USC College of Pharmacy in order to dramatically impact the personal and professional fulfillment of our graduates" (Kennedy Pharmacy Innovation Center Year in Review, 2021).

DESCRIPTION AND PURPOSE

The Kennedy Pharmacy Innovation Center is focused on innovation in the pharmacy field. Entering the pharmacist profession starts with the "core curriculum as a base for exploration and innovation, for elevating, enlarging and enhancing the role of pharmacy and pharmacists in an ever more challenging healthcare landscape" (About KPIC, n.d.). The programs offered at KPIC "prepare future pharmacists to pursue that dream in a collaborative, interdisciplinary environment that encourages ingenuity and innovation" (About KPIC, n.d.).

The Center brings the "nation's top minds in entrepreneurship, communications, health sciences, and other disciplines with leading pharmacy practice faculty, the hallmark and legacy of KPIC will be innovation in practice and education." Also, the "collaboration with the acclaimed Darla Moore School of Business for strong student support and entrepreneurship training escalates the culture of innovation" (About KPIC, n.d.).

DESCRIPTION OF CENTER OPERATIONS

The two core operations at KPIC include residency training and the Aseptic Compounding Experience (ACE) laboratory. The Center offers a Post Graduate Year (PGY), PGY-1 Residency Training program that "partners with community pharmacies in the Midlands area and provides a strong foundation in patient care along with valuable project management and professional development skills" (KPIC Year in Review, 2021).

A PGY-1/PGY 2 Community Based Pharmacy Administration and Leadership Residency program is also offered to "develop pharmacists who can provide high quality patient care, manage an innovative pharmacy practice, evaluate and improve the quality of care provided, lead organizational change, and advance the profession of pharmacy" (KPIC Year in Review, 2021).

ACE Laboratory

The ACE laboratory opened in 2014. It was created and "built partly in response to the 2012 fungal meningitis outbreak at a New England lab that killed 64 and sickened hundreds" (KPIC Year in Review, 2021). A meningitis outbreak was "traced to mold-tainted steroid injections produced by the company in Framingham Massachusetts, located about 20 miles (32 kilometers) west of Boston" (Richer, 2021). The outbreak highlighted "compounding pharmacies, which differ from ordinary drugstores in that they custom mix medications and supply them directly to hospitals and doctors" (Richer, 2021).

Prosecutors in the case said, "the facility cut corners to boost profits, neglected to properly disinfect its rooms, shipped drugs before receiving test results and ignored warning signs that its production methods were unsafe" (Richer, 2021). Pharmacists "who oversaw the facility's so-called clean rooms, were both acquitted of second-degree murder under the federal racketeering law but were found guilty of fraud, racketeering. and other crimes" (Richer, 2021).

KPIC was created to better train and equip pharmacy personnel in compounding activities. This groundbreaking lab was the "nation's first university-affiliated sterile medication compounding program, offering hands-on training, video technologies, coaching and end product testing" (KPIC Year in Review, 2021). This lab is "compliant with the highest national industry standards for sterile compounding, providing better training of future pharmacists, resulting in a significant impact on improved patient safety" (KPIC Year in Review, 2021).

Courses currently offered in the ACE lab include:

> Aseptic Technique Training Course: (7.5 hours home study, 16 hours live CE credit) This is a comprehensive, introductory sterile compounding training course . . .. Participants, who satisfactorily complete a program, receive a certificate of completion, as well as ACPE CE credits. This course was developed to train pharmacists and pharmacy technicians in aseptic technique and the basics of sterile compounding . . ..
>
> The course includes a home study component that will be completed by the participant prior to attending the workshop. The participant will also complete the core competencies required by current USP 797 standards in a state-of-the-art facility. (Sterile compounding CE courses, n.d.)

In addition, there are further courses offered:

Practical Compliance with USP Chapters 797 and 800 is an updated course geared towards individuals who are responsible for ensuring compliance with the USP Compounding Standards. The training is based on USP 797 (2019) version and current best practices.

The target audience includes pharmacists, pharmacy technicians, and others who are practicing in a sterile compounding environment and/or who are designated as responsible for the performance of a sterile compounding facility. Participants who satisfactorily complete the program will receive a certificate of completion. . .. (Sterile compounding CE courses, n.d.)

FURTHER FOCUS OF KPIC

Business Plan Competition

Other focus areas at KPIC include the Business Plan Competition, the Kennedy Career Enhancement Series, and the Pharmacy Ownership Boot Camp. The Business Plan Competition is offered to "help students develop a core component of being a successful entrepreneur" (KPIC Year in Review, 2021). The competition aids in student understanding of the "business planning process, allows for the design of creative practice models for the community pharmacy setting, with the goal of developing more pharmacy entrepreneurs" (KPIC Year in Review, 2021).

The competition includes "teams of up to four students that work with budgets, determine employee requirements, and develop a market and location analysis" (KPIC Year in Review, 2021). The winners of this competition go on to compete in the NCPA Student Business Plan and earn a scholarship.

Career Enhancement Series

The Kennedy Career Enhancement Series "consists of videos, webinars, infographics, and worksheets that help develop a career in pharmacy through networking, a catalog of professional meetings, job search, and discovering passion for the many available fields within pharmacy" (KPIC Year in Review, 2021). Networking includes the four traits of successful networkers: efficient, nimble, boundary-spanning, and energy-balanced. Also provided are tips on personal branding, successful elevator pitches, and LinkedIn (Kennedy Center Career Enhancement, n.d.).

Pharmacy Ownership Boot Camp

The Pharmacy Ownership Boot Camp is offered in conjunction with the National Community Pharmacists Association and is "specifically designed for pharmacy students and recent pharmacy graduates considering pharmacy ownership or desiring additional pharmacy financial management skills" (KPIC Year in Review, 2021). Those attending the boot camp "work with industry experts who share their knowledge and experience to help participants evaluate and prepare for potential careers in independent pharmacy ownership or management" (KPIC Year in Review, 2021).

Job Search Services

In the job search area, participants are provided with Curriculum Vitae and resume writing tips, cover letters, letters of intent writing techniques, requesting letters of recommendation, best practices for business cards, and interview advice. In the discovering passion focus, participants are encouraged to find their passion and explore ways to incorporate that passion into the pharmacy profession (Kennedy Career Enhancement Center, n.d.).

DESCRIPTION OF FACULTY, STAFF, AND STUDENTS

KPIC is led by the Executive Director, Dr. Patti Fabel. She is also a Clinical Associate Professor at the USC College of Pharmacy. She is a former president of the SC Pharmacy Association, involved with the American Pharmacist Association, and is president elect of the Academy of Pharmacy Practice and Management (APPM) for 2022–2023. Dr. Gene Reeder is the Director of Outcomes Research for KPIC and also Professor Emeritus at the USC College of Pharmacy. He is a 2015 recipient of the Distinguished Alumnus Award (About KPIC, n.d.).

Pamela Hite is a Global Certified Career Development Facilitator and the Program Coordinator at KPIC. There are also five lab interns employed by KPIC. These interns are pharmacy students enrolled at the college. There are six ACE lab Sterile Compounding Instructors. Dr. Nancy Roberts is the KPIC Sterile Compounding Training Program Director. Dr. Roberts has "practiced hospital pharmacy in two large teaching hospitals, a large VA hospital, both large and small community hospitals, and an oncology hospital" (About KPIC, n.d.).

Dr. Richard Capps is a KPIC Master Instructor with twenty-five plus years of experience in pharmacy management, including working with Greenville Health System hospitals and Oconee Memorial Hospital. He serves on ASHP committees and authored the chapter Primary Engineering Controls in ASHP's Compounding Sterile Preparations, 4th edition. Carl Dunn is a KPIC Master Instructor with over thirty years of experience, twenty-five years specializing in the hospital setting.

Shay Garrison is a KPIC Master Instructor with over thirty years of hospital experience, primarily at Palmetto Health Richland Hospital. Herman Watson is a KPIC Master Instructor with over forty years of experience in the hospital setting. Eric Sparks is a KPIC Master Instructor with over twenty years of experience in certification, calibration, and quality field as a metrologist. Sparks also "has managed many projects for major pharmaceutical manufacturers and sterile pharmacies, construction, air balancing, microbial sampling, calibration and certification within cleanrooms." (About KPIC, n.d.).

Connections to the USC College of Pharmacy

Many of the students at KPIC are pharmacy students enrolled at the USC College of Pharmacy. With KPIC offices being housed on the second floor and the ACE lab in the basement, there is a close relationship with the school and center. Most of the programmatic offerings are aimed at future pharmacists. However, there are some education opportunities for pharmacy support staff. Pharmacy technicians can take courses on aseptic technique and hazardous drugs. These courses are continuing education courses that earn CE credits for annual SC Board of Pharmacy license renewal.

DESCRIPTION OF CENTER OUTCOMES

KPIC was designed for creating and innovating new roles for pharmacists. The Center participates in the Flip the Pharmacy Initiative. This initiative "aims to transform community-based pharmacies away from point-in-time, prescription level care processes and business models to longitudinal and patient level care processes and business models that are both replicable and sustainable" (KPIC Year in Review, 2021).

STRENGTHS AND IMPROVEMENTS

The most significant strength noted at KPIC is the ongoing commitment to innovation. Pharmacy students are being prepared for the careers of the future, not the current employment landscape. They are encouraged to find new ways to practice pharmacy and incorporate their individual passions into their work to make it meaningful to themselves and their future patients. Another strength is the commitment to connect with alumni. Current students benefit from being on campus in the same building with KPIC. Faculty and staff are committed to also engaging with alumni to provide training for the new career paths available in the future.

The main suggestion for improvement is to welcome other pharmacy staff into the center. The majority of the programs are geared toward pharmacists and pharmacy students. This is advantageous for these groups but could leave the support staff confused about their place at KPIC. Those currently in the field know that pharmacy technicians are welcome to participate any of the continuing education offerings at the Center, but newly registered technicians may view the website and not notice the opportunities that are afforded to them.

VALUE FOR STUDENTS

KPIC value for students is great. Graduating pharmacy students who have participated in the various KPIC course and competition offerings are vastly more prepared than traditional pharmacy school graduates to be innovators and entrepreneurs. Not only are resumes built, valuable skills are gained to help them create new areas of practice.

VALUE FOR SERVICE AREA

The general service area for KPIC is South Carolina. As of 2019, there were 4,827 practicing pharmacists and 7,009 practicing pharmacy technicians (South Carolina Health Professions Data Book, 2019). Given the opportunity to provide continuing education to over 11,000 pharmacy professionals, there is great value to the SC area.

With the focus of both community and hospital practice settings, course offerings will appeal to a variety of audiences. The service area is not limited to South Carolina. KPIC offers their ACE lab aseptic technique and hazardous drug courses to pharmacists and pharmacy technicians nationwide. Students have come from multiple states to be trained in the state-of-the-art facility at KPIC.

KPIC also partners with local technical colleges to offer aseptic technique training in the ACE lab. Midlands Technical College had a partnership with KPIC to train enrolled pharmacy technician students in the lab alongside other pharmacy professionals. The two-day training was completed with over twenty hours of continuing education credits earned toward SC Board registration the following year. Students were taught in a fully compliant USP 797 sterile compounding pharmacy lab space and passed fingertip sampling and media fill testing requirements.

FUTURE OF CENTER

The future of KPIC is encouraging. Program Coordinator Pamela Hite shared that the Center is focused on increasing its reach and impact, sustainability and growth, increasing educational offerings, and non-traditional practice models (P. Hite, personal communication, June 18, 2021). These areas support the KPIC vision that the "USC College of Pharmacy is the recognized leader in transforming pharmacy education and practice" (About KPIC, n.d.).

Executive Director Fabel noted that the Center is "building upon a strong foundation thanks to the talented professionals who have led and worked with KPIC in the past" (Gamecock Pharmacist, 2018). Her plans are to "continue the enhance the knowledge and education experiences of our students while serving as a bridge to connect students with our talented alumni." Fabel noted that "we are here not only to educate our students but to inspire them as well. . .we want to broaden career opportunities for students and alumni" (Gamecock Pharmacist, 2018).

KPIC will help by showing "students how to differentiate themselves and sharpen their skills so they can create their own jobs beyond traditional career opportunities" (Gamecock Pharmacist, 2018). KPIC is interested in showcasing non-traditional career paths such as "consulting and embedding pharmacies within medical practices. Fabel stated that "the Kennedy Center could step in and provide connection opportunities to areas such as regulatory affairs, sterile compounding manufacturing, or help them develop necessary skills to blaze a new career path" (Gamecock Pharmacist, 2018).

CONCLUSION

KPIC is a unique organization with innovation at its core. It has chosen to be a trailblazing education institution with a focus on new and emerging fields in pharmacy practice. The profession of pharmacy can be so much more than a prescription pick up experience. With pharmacists being embedded in local communities, advanced and expanded health care is on the horizon with the new and innovative fields being explored at KPIC.

REFERENCES

About KPIC. (n.d.). Retrieved from https://kennedycenter.sc.edu/about-kpic/our-vision Gamecock Pharmacist. (2018). University of South Carolina Publishing, Columbia, SC.

Kennedy Career Enhancement Center. (n.d.). Retrieved from https://kennedycenter.sc.edu/kennedy-career-enhancement-series

Kennedy Pharmacy Innovation Center Year in Review. (2021). University of South Carolina Publishing, Columbia, SC.

Richer, A. D. (July 7, 2021). *Pharmacy exec sentenced to 14 years in Meningitis outbreak.* Retrieved from https://abcnews.go.com/Health/wire-Story/pharmacy-exec-resentenced-14-years-meningitis-outbreak-78714758

South Carolina Health Professions Data Book. (2019). Retrieved from https://www.scohw.org/docs/2019/SCOHW-Data-Book-2019.pdf

Sterile Compounding CE Courses. (n.d.). Retrieved from https://kennedycenter.sc.edu/sterile-compounding/sterile-compounding-training-programs

Chapter 11

Center of Excellence for University Teaching

Amber Lennon-Harmon

At any given point during the lifespan of an organization, there will be challenges that arise threatening the longevity of the organization. From nimble startups, fortune 500 companies to institutions of higher education, it has been proven that driving value, innovation, and adaptability are the cornerstones of long-term success. Most organizations that are failing to rapidly innovate are suffering because of a lack of access to expertise. Thus, at some point in time, organizations are able to benefit from the development and effective implementation of a Center of Excellence (Wright, M. et al., 2018).

The priorities of a Center of Excellence vary across industries and can be expected to change over time with the growth and development of the organization. According to Perficient "a center of excellence is a (typically small) team of dedicated individuals managed from a common central point, separate from the functional areas that it supports within a practice or organization" (Perficient, n.d., p. 3). These centers enable organizations to hone their expertise in specific areas, standardize best practices, and provide direction and thought leadership in their area of expertise.

When specifically looking at institutions of higher education, Centers of Excellence provide the framework for exploring and adopting new practices, techniques, and technology as a means of achieving the institution's mission and vision and ultimately impacting the students served by the institution. This chapter will provide an overview of the Center for Teaching Excellence and Faculty Leadership at The University of North Carolina Wilmington.

OVERVIEW OF THE UNIVERSITY OF NORTH CAROLINA WILMINGTON

The University of North Carolina (UNC) System is a multi-campus system comprised of sixteen universities and the NC School of Science and Mathematics. The UNC System has a long history of a formal teaching role in addition to a strong commitment to public service and research. Instruction, research, and outreach and service are the three components of the system's mission. The mission "is to discover, create, transmit, and apply knowledge to address the needs of individuals and society" (UNC System, 2021).

Formerly known as Wilmington College, the university was founded in 1947 to provide higher educational opportunities to students in southeastern North Carolina and joined the UNC system in 1969.

Located on the coast of North Carolina in the city of Wilmington, The University of North Carolina Wilmington (UNCW) is home to over 17,000 undergraduate and graduate students and just under 2,500 faculty and staff members. UNCW offers fifty-six bachelor's degree programs, thirty-six master's degree programs, and four doctoral programs. In fall 2019, UNCW became the first university in the nation to offer a Bachelor of Science degree in Coastal Engineering.

University Mission

The mission of the university is to integrate "teaching and mentoring with research and service" (University of North Carolina Wilmington, 2021a). The university is committed to student engagement, creative inquiry, critical thinking, thoughtful expression, and responsible citizenship and values excellence, diversity, integrity, student-centered focus, community engagement, and innovation. UNCW aims to be recognized "for excellence in everything it does, for its global mindset and for its community engagement" (University of North Carolina Wilmington, 2021a).

The university's values in addition to its dedication to community engagement serve as the bedrock of their 2016–2022 strategic plan to guide their future growth. Under the leadership of Chancellor Jose Sartarelli, UNCW continues to be recognized and acknowledged for its world-class faculty, staff, affordability, and academic excellence.

PURPOSE AND OPERATION OF THE UNCW CENTER FOR TEACHING EXCELLENCE AND FACULTY LEADERSHIP

The Center for Teaching Excellence (CTE) and the Center for Faculty Leadership (CFL) partner with ten campus units in order to provide a variety of professional development opportunities in teaching and leadership for faculty and staff members at UNCW.

These campus partnerships include Undergraduate Studies, The Graduate School, The Honors College, Applied Learning, Office of International Programs, The Career Center, The Office of Student Leadership and Engagement, Quality Enhancement for Nonprofit Organization, Colonial Academic Alliance, and the Office of E-Learning.

Both centers participate in national and state associations that provide professional development opportunities in teaching which support the overall mission of improving higher education. The CTE and CFL also participate in formal and informal resource-sharing consortia within the University of North Carolina system. The Center for Teaching Excellence is "dedicated to assisting the University in fulfilling its commitment to strengthening undergraduate and graduate instruction" (UNCW, 2021b).

The development of new courses and the improvement of existing courses are two of the fundamental needs of maintaining the integrity and vitality of the educational programs offered by UNC Wilmington. The CTE realizes that "excellence in teaching is only achieved through teaching scholarship, which involves continuous scrutiny of course content and methods of instruction, knowledge of modern educational techniques and practices, and analysis of the effects of different teaching methods on student learning" (UNCW, 2021b).

Participation by faculty is entirely voluntary and interactions between faculty and the Center's personnel is completely confidential and is separate from any formal assessment process of UNCW.

Mission of the Center

The mission of the center is to "foster a campus-wide climate where teaching is highly valued, as well as provide leadership in the application of scholarship to teaching" (UNCW, 2021b). The Center also believes that it is the primary responsibility of the faculty to develop and improve educational programs as they possess the skills and knowledge needed to evaluate and implement effective instructional practices.

In tandem with the Center for Teaching Excellence, the Center for Faculty Leadership is "dedicated to developing and sustaining a high quality of academic leadership that is central to the mission and goals outlined in the University's strategic plan" (UNCW, 2021c).

The CFL is multifunctional as it provides resources and support for individuals interested in academic leadership roles, serves as a training center for newly appointed department chairs, division coordinators, and program directors, and offers retooling opportunities for leaders who are interested in improving the quality of academic programs being offered or those interested in seeking higher leadership roles within the University's administration.

"Information and assistance emphasize exploration, experimentation, and networking with programs presented in a variety of venues: informal discussions, formal workshops, guest speakers, conference, networking, and alliance building, mentoring and shadowing" (UNCW, 2021c). Additionally, the center encourages collaborative initiatives by the faculty at UNCW.

Center Faculty

The CTE and CFL is led by a small but mighty group of educators who are dedicated to supporting UNCW faculty and providing ample professional development and learning opportunities to enhance the learning experiences for students. Diana Ashe, PhD serves as the director for the center and also serves as an associate professor for the Department of English, where she has worked since 2000. In her role as the director, she provides leadership support and orientation to all thirty-eight department chairs and school Directors at UNCW.

Matthew TenHuisen, PhD, is an associate professor in the mathematics department and serves as the Associate Director of the center. He previously served as the Chair of the Mathematics and Statistics department. In his role as the Associate Director, he conducts new faculty development work and works closely with Chairs and Directors.

Colleen Reilly, PhD, is a professor in the English department and serves as the Applied Learning Faculty Associate. Reilly has a background working with the UNC system's statewide Faculty Assembly and its Executive Council and brings an understanding of trends and challenges in higher education which directly impacts the centers' faculty development efforts. Additionally, there is an Advisory Board in place to support both centers. The board is composed of over ten faculty and staff members from a variety of departments and disciplines across the campus.

OVERVIEW OF STUDENTS, FACULTY, AND STAFF

In an effort to improve and enhance data availability and transparency at UNCW, the Institutional Research and Planning Office has developed interactive data visualizations and dashboards. According to their student achievement and graduation rate dashboards, for the fall 2019 full-time cohort, the retention rate of students was 86.2 percent and there was a 79.1 percent graduation rate.

Student Enrollment

Based upon the fall 2020 enrollment data, the total enrollment of students at UNCW was 17,915 with 14,650 being undergraduate students. Of the 2,025 new freshmen at UNCW, 63 percent were female and 37 percent were male students with 86 percent of students enrolling from the state of North Carolina. South Eastern Carolina residents of New Hanover, Pender, Brunswick, Columbus, Bladen, Sampson, Duplin, and Onslow counties made up 14 percent of the North Carolina student population.

Faculty

UNCW employs 1,055 faculty members, and 1,424 staff members. UNCW faculty, staff, and students are actively involved and engaged in research resulting in a regional, national, and global impact. "Since 2017, the university has hosted two Global Marine Science Summits that brought scholars and other experts from around the world to the UNCW campus" (UNCW, 2021c).

The faculty at UNCW conduct stellar research programs and partner with students to explore a number of fields to include the arts and humanities, educational leadership, data sciences, health and wellness, coastal and marine environments, aquaculture, and drug development.

During the 2018–2019 fiscal year, researchers from UNCW secured over twelve million dollars in sponsored funding. The amazing research being conducted at UNCW is directly tied to the university's mission while impacting the region's economic vitality through the creation of new innovative businesses, job development, and the discovery of new services and products.

STRENGTHS AND CHALLENGES OF THE CENTER

In an interview with the CTE and CFL director, Dr. Ashe, it was evident that the director is extremely passionate about the work that she does at UNCW in this capacity. While there are many qualities that can be attributed to an effective leader, passion for students and for the services provided are extremely important, especially during tough times such as the COVID-19 pandemic. One of the strengths of the center is the pure passion for the work. As the team UNCW is small, it is evident that their passion about helping faculty members enhance their skill sets is what drives their success.

During the interview one of the most fascinating topics discussed was how the director encourages faculty members to participate in professional development opportunities that are unrelated to their subject areas of expertise. The reasoning behind this is to allow faculty members to fully understand what it feels like to be introduced to new concepts and subjects and experience failure.

For example, for a student who has never taken an economics course, the material is brand new and may seem daunting, the same way in which a professor who has never taken a ceramics class would feel uncomfortable. This simple experience allows faculty members to think intentionally about how they think about their course content and delivery methods. (D. Ashe, personal communication, June 24, 2021)

Another strength is the intentionality of forming communities among UNCW faculty and staff members. According to Dr. Ashe, "the unspoken motto of the center and the reasoning behind their work is to foster and support intentional communities of faculty" (D. Ashe, personal communication, June 24, 2021). When faculty, staff, and academic leaders are in sync, all students are provided with a more robust student learning experience.

As the student population of UNCW continues to grow, it will be more critical for faculty and staff to work collaboratively to discuss and understand issues related to teaching, learning, and leadership. Many faculty members have been recognized for their amazing contributions to research. Thus, the timely and effective faculty development opportunities improve all aspects of the campus community.

Challenge to the Center

On the other hand, the largest challenge faced by the center is that it is understaffed. At this time all faculty developers are tenured faculty, operating at 1.9 faculty developers for 1,000 faculty members. Not only is this small but mighty team running two centers, but the core leadership team are also faculty members. While this serves as a strength it is also a challenge as they all have faculty responsibilities in addition to the work that they do for the centers. Dr. Ashe and Dr. TenHuisen are split 70/30 and Dr. Reilly is split 50/50 in regards to the work they do with the centers and responsibilities as faculty members.

It would be helpful to have additional full-time staff or additional contracted staff members to alleviate some of the workload shared by the team. Another challenge to the center is not having the detailed reports of the center's contributions to the university. With dwindling budgets and more of a focus on fundraising and this would be a great time to create reports and dashboards outlining the impact of the center on the campus community as a means of generating additional revenue for the center to expand offerings available for faculty.

Lastly, as technology continues to advance it will be important to maintain updated websites that are easy to navigate to ensure equal accessibility for faculty and staff searching for resources and support from the centers. Dr. Ashe mentioned that the CTE and CFL website has not been updated recently as so much of their time and effort has been spent on updating and maintaining the *Keep Teaching* website (D. Ashe, personal communication, June 24, 2021). In the future, it would be helpful to have a full-time position dedicated to updating and maintaining the center's website to alleviate this responsibility from the rest of the staff.

VALUE OF THE CENTER FOR STUDENTS AND INSTITUTION'S SERVICE AREA

As many institutions of higher education spend a large amount of time, energy, and resources to develop and enhance student success initiatives, residence life programs, and student engagement opportunities for students, it is important to recognize the huge impact that faculty members have in the lives of students.

Historically, the value of a college education was directly linked to job and graduate school data and alumni salaries and not based on a holistic view of the college experience. In 2014, Gallup and Purdue University focused their efforts on researching the common and essential experiences of college students no matter the type of institution they attended.

Polls

Gallup and Purdue designed an index examining the long-term success of graduates after graduation further explaining the relationship between the lived college experience and life after graduation. This index outlined six main collegiate experiences. The experience with the highest percentage characterizing the undergraduate student experience, was that the student had at least one professor who made them excited about learning.

Extracurricular activities, experiential learning, and real-world class projects all add to the overall collegiate experience but the fact remains that faculty members are at the core of the students' learning experience (Seymour, S. and Lopez, S., 2015).

The CTE partnered with the Office for Distance Education and eLearning (DEeL) to develop a *Keep Teaching* website, which has been made available for UNCW faculty and staff. As many unplanned situations including the global COVID-19 pandemic require the implementation of new and existing technologies to continue teaching, this website provides resources and support to UNCW faculty. The website was developed as a means to provide necessary resources and guidelines enabling faculty to teach from a distance and in those instances where students are unable to attend their classes in-person.

In addition to teaching resources, strategies, and training and development calendars, the website includes an entire section dedicated to faculty wellness. This is important to point out as so many college students are suffering with mental health issues. In order to support students during their college experiences, it is also important for faculty members to focus on their personal wellness in order to be effective in their role on campus. The inclusion and emphasis placed on wellness adds huge value to students as their experience in the classroom whether in-person or online is enhanced when faculty members are well.

UNCW is known as the University of North Carolina system's coastal university and serves most of southeastern North Carolina. The university's dedication to teaching, mentoring, research, and service can be seen in the number of rankings and recognitions that have been received. UNCW has been ranked among the best regional universities in the south by the *U.S. News & World Report* and it was also named to the 2015 list of best southeastern schools by *The Princeton Review.*

One of the most impressive rankings that truly shows the value add to students and the university's service area is that the university ranked among the top ten four-year public universities with the most impressive gains in graduation rates nationally. Additionally, UNCW has made significant progress towards bridging the gap between white and underrepresented minority six-year graduation rates.

FUTURE OF THE CENTER

Institutions of higher education across the world were faced with a number of challenges due to the COVID-19 pandemic. Aside from ensuring the health and safety of faculty, staff, and students, most institutions were faced with quickly transitioning traditional in-person courses to an online format. This quick shift posed a number of challenges including a lack of technical resources and digital skills needed to effectively teach virtually. While virtual learning presents its own set of challenges, the future of institutions of higher education and the accessibility of online learning is here to stay.

Ashe discussed how the center was able to offer an increased number of workshops to support faculty members with the transition to online learning and were able to help faculty members rethink their course syllabi. The future of the CTE and CFL will most definitely include increased efforts to support online learning and even hybrid classes (D. Ashe, personal communication, June 24, 2021).

Additionally, as previously mentioned, the centers will need to focus on using existing data to inform decision-making. As the centers are currently not expected to create and distribute annual reports of the center's usage and movement toward internal strategic goals, it will be important for the staff to make this a priority to ensure that the needs of the faculty members are being met and most importantly that the work that is being done is effective, and intentional. With such a small administrative team, it will be important to maximize the time, talent, and available resources to support long-term success of the centers.

During the interview with Dr. Ashe, she discussed that over the course of the last year the center was able to offer ninety-nine programs for faculty members as they transitioned to online learning. It was clear that this would not be a sustainable goal in the future with such a small staff. Thus, the documentation of the center's offering along with a detailed outline of the time and resources needed to operate at a high level will be needed to advocate for additional staff members and resources in the future to support the centers (D. Ashe, personal communication, June 24, 2021).

CONCLUSION

The development and implementation of a Center of Excellence at an institution of higher education will vary based on the needs, resources, and support available to the institution. However, as the needs of students and student demographics across all college campuses continues to change and become more diverse, effective Centers of Excellence will be critical to the success of higher education institutions. As the impacts of the COVID-19 pandemic forced institutions to quickly adapt to a virtual learning setting, institutions of higher education now have the responsibility of educating students in a number of ways in this new digital age.

This transition requires faculty members to be qualified and equipped with the digital competencies needed to effectively teach students. Higher education institutions have a huge responsibility of effectively preparing faculty for this transition. UNCW's Center for Teaching Excellence and Center for Faculty Leadership allows faculty and staff to work collaboratively and share ideas and strategies. This ultimately helps everyone save time and energy while engaging all students in their own learning experiences.

Centers of Teaching Excellence provide a place of intellectual collegiality and supports the meaningful work of faculty members. When the needs of faculty are being met and they are provided with ample resources and support, there will be an increased motivation to learn and apply new knowledge leading to enhanced learning environments for students.

REFERENCES

Perficient. (n.d.). Five guiding principles of a successful center of excellence. Retrieved from https://www.perficient.com/-/media/files/guide-pdf-links/five-guiding-principles-of-a-successful-center-of-excellence.pdf

Seymour,S., Lopez,S. (2015). Big six college experiences linked to life preparedness. Gallup. Retrieved from https://news.gallup.com/poll/182306/big-six-college-experiences-linked-life-preparedness.aspx

The University of North Carolina System (2021). Our mission. *About Us*. Retrieved from https://www.northcarolina.edu/about-us/

The University of North Carolina Wilmington (2021a). About us. Retrieved from https://uncw.edu/aboutuncw/facts.html

The University of North Carolina Wilmington (2021b). The center for teaching excellence. Retrieved from https://uncw.edu/cte/about.html

The University of North Carolina Wilmington (2021c). Center for faculty leadership. Retrieved from https://uncw.edu/cte/facultyleadership.html

Wright, M., Lohe, D., & Little, D. (2018). The role of a center for teaching and learning in a de-centered educational world. *Change: The Magazine of Higher Learning. 50* (6), 38–44.

Chapter 12

Center of Excellence for Manufacturing and Technology

Lauren Holland

The Southeastern Institute of Manufacturing and Technology is an advanced manufacturing center designed to support workforce and economic development, as well as provide a home for training students and supporting the launch of new products. It is located on the main campus of Florence-Darlington Technical College (FDTC), a mid-size community college of approximately 4,000 curriculum students, located in Florence, South Carolina. Darlington and Marion Counties also comprise the college service area.

Florence's location at the halfway mark between New York and Miami, as well as its position at the crossroads of Interstate 95 and Interstate 20 make it an attractive place for manufacturers to locate, given the ease with which they can receive and ship goods. The relatively new Inland Port, located in nearby Dillon, adds to the appeal of the Florence location for manufacturers, as well. The Inland Port uses rail to provide import and export services to industry, and it directly serves 100 foreign ports, providing a cost-effective means for tracking empty containers and returning them loaded and ready for export (South Carolina Ports Authority website, n.d.).

BACKGROUND AND PURPOSE

The concept of the SiMT was developed by FDTC's former president, Dr. Charles Gould, who recognized during his tenure a need for the institution to generate non-traditional revenue, in light of the growing decrease in funding for colleges. The SiMT was designed to create business units in cutting edge technology, each of which would contribute badly needed revenue to the institution. That revenue is directly tied to the mission of the center. The SiMT supports FDTC's students, and the college as a whole, as it produces funds for scholarships, equipment, and other institutional needs.

The money generated by the SiMT is non-restrictive, in that it can be used for any objectives at FDTC, unlike other funding sources, which are restricted for certain purposes, such as equipment or facilities maintenance. The SiMT is an actual division of FDTC, with an appointed Vice President, who oversees operations. As such, it is considered a state agency, and thereby subject to all state rules and regulations on purchasing, procurement, and financial activities (SiMT, n.d.).

SIMT OPERATIONS AND STAFF

The Facility

Currently, the SiMT has five business units. The facility, itself, is one business unit, and presently is the unit that, pre-COVID-19, produced the most income for the college. The SiMT boasts an 800-seat auditorium, an impressive lobby designed with moveable furniture, so that it can accommodate large receptions, a conference center, and abundant classroom space.

Customers have rented the lobby and conference center for weddings and tradeshows, and local businesses frequently rent classroom space for training or other events. The auditorium hosts a number of events each year, including dance recitals and other community happenings. The facilities unit is managed by Anna Lane, who is known for her excellent customer service, and who manages a staff of three other individuals to run facilities operations.

Additive Manufacturing

Additive manufacturing is a procedure by which objects are created through the layering process of materials. Additive manufactured products may be created out of a variety of materials, but most often include plastics or metals. The benefits of additive manufacturing, more commonly known as 3-D printing, are many. Primarily, additive manufacturing allows for a broader freedom in design in prototypes. It also is more cost-efficient, when small batches of a product are needed, or for when a product needs to be highly customized (Boyd, 2016).

Additive Manufacturing is the second business unit of the SiMT. It provides rapid prototyping for entrepreneurs, a service which enables them to quickly bring a new product to market for testing. Rapid prototyping significantly reduces the amount of time needed to produce a prototype. The unit also supports budding businesses by acting as a sole source provider for products, resulting in a start-up business's ability to operate with reduced space and a smaller workforce, each of which are common challenges to new businesses (SiMT, n.d.).

The Additive Manufacturing center has effectively demonstrated its ability to support innovation in the healthcare industry, as well. Several years ago, the unit worked with physicians who were treating a soldier, who had been shot in his head, during combat. An image of the soldier's skull was scanned and delivered to the Additive Manufacturing Center. The Center produced a 3-D model of the skull, allowing the physicians to configure, before scheduling the operation to remove the bullet, the best way to surgically enter the soldier's skull.

In addition, having the printed model of the skull permitted the surgeons the opportunity build a mesh piece that would be fitted into the skull, as part of operation, and to confidently know, pre-surgery, that it would fit properly (Steven Broach, personal communication, October 10, 2020). Both the Additive Manufacturing Center and the Advanced Machining Center are managed by Jonathan Melton, a seasoned machinist with a solid manufacturing background.

Advanced Machining

The Advanced Machining unit provides machine part services to businesses and innovators. Services of this unit include machined parts with complex geometries and close tolerances, as well as creating parts that meet specifications required for formal testing or production on a large scale. The advanced machining staff also often partner with the additive manufacturing unit, to produce working prototypes of new products (*Advanced machining*, n.d.).

One successful company who took advantage of the Advanced Machining unit at the SiMT was a start-up called Growler Chill, a manufacturer of countertop refrigeration units for beer growlers. The Advanced Machining unit produced several small internal components for the Growler Chill unit.

The most recently added additions to the repertoire of the SiMT services are the Gould Business Incubator and the Social Media Listening Center. The incubator serves to support entrepreneurship and the launching of start-up companies, by making available office space and business services. Mark Roth, Vice President of the SiMT, said in an October 2020 discussion that 94percent of the new companies who have begun their inception at the incubator, were still in business (Mark A. Roth, personal communication, October 10, 2020).

One of the most successful companies to emerge from the Gould Incubator is Ben-No-Mo. The company's name is jargon for "Bend No More," (Ben No Mo website, n.d.), and the company produces a product that originally was used to prevent individuals from having to continuously bend over to retrieve beverages from a cooler on the ground.

The Ben No Mo product is a collapsible, adjustable stand, which has morphed into also serving as a receptacle for toolboxes and campfire grills, as well. Ben No Mo was the first manufacturer to incubate in the Gould Incubator, and its owners have expressed much gratitude to the SiMT, for its success (Ben No Mo website, n.d.).

On the Ben No Mo website, the following is written:

> We are thankful for the Gould Business Incubator on the SiMT campus at Florence-Darlington Technical College for providing the support and manufacturing space to help us launch our product. The Ben No-Mo was the first manufacturing business to lease space in the Incubator and we're proud to be part of such an incredible institution of learning. (Ben No Mo website, n.d., About Section Para. 6)

The Gould Incubator also supports local economic development, by successfully contributing to the creation of new businesses, which create jobs and pay taxes.

Social Media Listening Center

The Social Media Listening Center is the youngest SiMT unit. This center supports new businesses and product launches by providing a means to tap into, and manage and monitor, the powerful technology of social media. Platforms for social media are used to propel new products into the marketplace, and social media is a much more effective way to advertise, than the traditional means of print media and television. The Social Media Listening Center can also provide monitoring services, in which it captures all mention of topics, products, or ideas, across the World Wide Web.

Sonoco, a major manufacturer of packaging solutions, used the Social Media Listening Center when its flexible packaging division launched the squeezable tube container for Daisy Sour Cream. Sonoco utilized the services of the Center to gauge consumer response to the new packaging, and to test its likeability. One niche market that has recently developed in the Center is the monitoring of potential online threats for school systems and college campuses.

A recent contract was secured by the Center to closely monitor threats pertaining to the Florence County District 1 School System, in Florence, South Carolina. Duane Childers, with experience in the field of print media, is the manager assigned to the Social Media Listening Center.

The SiMT is managed and supervised by Dr. Mark Roth, Vice President, and Tressa Gardner, Associate Vice President. Prior to entering higher education, Dr. Roth was a successful entrepreneur, having started numerous companies, and a successful businessman in the private sector. Tressa Gardner brings a solid business and manufacturing background to the SiMT's management team.

FACULTY, STAFF, AND STUDENTS

Three FDTC academic programs are housed within the SiMT. These are Industrial Maintenance, Machine Tool Technology, and Engineering. Having these located within the SiMT is ideal, as these programs are most closely associated with the primary business and industries located in the college service area. When prospective or existing business or industry leaders visit the SiMT, they can see first-hand the

Industrial Maintenance and Machine Tool Technology students in training, through the large glass partition that offers a view into the SiMT's arena, where hands on training for these students occurs. The arena allows for business and industry leaders to also intersperse among students, while they are in training, to quiz them on what they are learning, and to scout for potential recruits for interns, apprentices, or future workers. Students are told that when they see Tressa Gardner, Associate Vice President for the SiMT, walking around with visitors, they should be on their best professional behavior, as most likely, the visitor is a future potential employer. Faculty offices and classrooms for Industrial Maintenance, Machine Tool Technology, and Engineering are also located at the SiMT.

Having these housed under one roof further supports the SiMT and local workforce and economic development. A recent new development is the beginning of a healthcare simulation laboratory, under the college's Corporate and Workforce Development division, in the space formerly occupied by the SiMT's virtual reality studio. A staff person with the Corporate and Workforce Development division has acquired the zSpace units, which are used to provide interactive virtual reality experiences at a desktop (zSpace website, n.d.).

These are being used to teach human anatomy to the college's first Emergency Medical Technician (EMT) apprentices for a local ambulance services provider. The zSpace technology permits students to view and manipulate, in a 3-D environment, a human body, and reinforces what they learn in the classroom about the location and function of organs and other anatomy. The virtual reality studio also had acquired a Milo range theater system.

This system allows for a fully immersive training environment, and was initially created to be used to train law enforcement in rapid responses to simulated environments, where participants have a 180-degree view of the simulation.

The Milo Range also contains simulated environments in healthcare and emergency response scenarios (Milo Range website, n.d.), and is also being deployed to teach the EMT apprentices. The Corporate and Workforce Development division has requested in its budget for next year funds to purchase an ambulance simulator, which will also support new technology for teaching EMTs. The zSpace, Milo Range, and ambulance simulator are located within the former virtual reality studio, and they are expected to be the healthcare simulation lab for workforce development.

EXPECTED OUTCOMES FOR THE SIMT

The major expected outcome associated with the SiMT, as was the initial vision of Dr. Charles Gould, is to produce additional, needed revenue for the college. Its business units do that, as does the college's Corporate and Workforce Development division, which while not a true component of the SiMT, is located within the facility, and reports under the SiMT's vice president.

A secondary outcome for the center is to train and produce graduates who will be equipped with skills to support workforce development needs within the college service area. The three academic programs located within the SiMT, Industrial Maintenance, Engineering, and Machine Tool Technology, all contribute to that endeavor, as does the Corporate and Workforce Development division. It is also expected that the SiMT will continue to be a shining star in the state, and help recruit and support new business and industry in the region.

STRENGTHS AND WEAKNESSES

The SiMT excels in the individuals that have been hired to manage its units. Each have strong credentials and experience in their respective fields, and those are parlayed into the creative and excellent services provided by the SiMT. The Additive Manufacturing Center stands out, as it has the broadest capacity of additive manufacturing services on the east coast, and it has the ability to 3-D print in a wide variety of metals and colors. The Gould Incubator is cleared to produce considerable revenue each year, which is its greatest contribution to the college, thus far (Patressa Gardner, personal communication, May 11, 2021).

Another institution of higher education in the area, Francis Marion University, has recently opened its own incubator, and the SiMT facilities unit recently lost an annual event that drew approximately 5,000 visitors, and which was its largest customer each year, to the local civic center (Patressa Gardner, personal communication, May 11, 2021).

ANALYSIS OF VALUE TO STUDENTS

One value to students in the FDTC Machine Tool Technology, Industrial Maintenance, and Engineering programs is opportunities for prospective employment by the number of business and industry visitors to the center each year. Each of these visitors represent a potential future employer, with a vested interest in filling his or her talent pipeline.

When they visit the SiMT, they witness students learning, and often have the opportunity to engage with students, and scout for potential new talent. Students also have the opportunity to be exposed to cutting technology in one of the business units, which they may use in a future career, related to their program of study.

ANALYSIS OF VALUE TO COLLEGE SERVICE AREA

Also housed within the SiMT is the Florence County Economic Development offices. The Florence County economic development team, as well as that of Darlington and Marion Counties, each frequently bring prospective businesses that they are recruiting to the SiMT. The SiMT's presence alone, is commanding and makes an excellent impression on prospective industries who are considering setting up operations in the college's service area. Potential new employers can witness how the SiMT business units can assist in their operations, but they may also see firsthand their future workforce being trained, as well.

In addition, the SiMT brings a multitude of visitors to the center, from both nearby locations, as well as from around the world. Sonoco, a global manufacturer of packaging solutions, is located in nearby Hartsville, which is in the college's service area, and it rents the entire SiMT once a year, to host its corporate meetings, which are attended by many international Sonoco associates. The SiMT is a source of local and state pride, and is the envy of many other South Carolina technical colleges.

THE SIMT'S FUTURE

The SiMT and its management team might also consider how the Fourth Industrial Revolution will impact the center's operations. Big data is providing ways to increase productivity within metalworking, and machine shop operators who do not prepare may get left behind (Jahn, 2019). The craving for big data among business and industry presents another future opportunity for the SiMT. Since 2012, opportunities for data scientists have experienced a growth rate of more than 650%, and data science positions consistently rank as one of the most in demand occupations (Future of Data Science, n.d.).

Future Plans

The SiMT might consider in the future adding a business unit that can support data science needs by area employers, and possibly a program to award certificates in this growing area. As with data science, the SiMT's senior leadership and its business unit managers would do well to consider its impact and that of the Fourth Industrial Revolution technologies, and begin preparing now for how to make sure their gem of an advanced manufacturing center stays current in technology. The rapid pace with which technology is changing manufacturing could present opportunities, as well as challenges, for the SiMT in the future.

CONCLUSION

The SiMT has a commanding presence in the state of South Carolina, and it is valued for a myriad of reasons within the FDTC community. If carefully managed, and if alternate sources of revenue can be secured, perhaps through a network of salespeople, the center could continue to thrive, especially as technology transforms manufacturing processes. The center has provided a number of valuable services to entrepreneurs, students, faculty, and economic development officials over the years, and contributes significantly to local workforce and economic development, as well as to FDTC students and the larger community.

REFERENCES

Advanced machining center. (n.d.). Retrieved from SiMT website: https://simt.sc.gov/sites/default/files/Documents/Advanced_Machining_Brochure.pdf

Ben No Mo website. (n.d.). http://www.ben-no-mo.com

Boyd, P. (2016). These industries are the future of additive manufacturing. Retrieved from https://www.industryweek.com/technology-and-iiot/emerging-technologies/article/22006101/these-industries-are-the-future-of-additive-manufacturing

Jahn, U. (2019). Machining, disruption, and the years ahead. Retrieved from https://www.mmsonline.com/articles/machining-disruption-and-the-years-ahead-

Manufacturers' Agents National Association. (n.d.). https://www.manaonline.org/

Milo Range website. (n.d.) https://www.faac.com/milo/virtual/milo-range-theater/

SiMT. (n.d.). https://simt.sc.gov/about-us

South Carolina Ports Authority website. (n.d.) https://scspa.com/locations/inland-port-dillon/

Steven Broach, personal communication, October 10, 2020.

What does the future of data science hold. (n.d.) Retrieved from https://www.elmhurst.edu/blog/future-of-data-science/

zSpace website. (n.d.). https://zspace.com/technology

Epilogue

The results from the research into Centers of Excellence by graduate students at Wingate University, demonstrate that the topics pursued result from local needs identified by specific institutions of higher education. The various topics included in this book, international studies, energy regulation, biotechnology, advanced manufacturing, cybersecurity, agricultural interests, pharmacy, business, teaching and learning seem to have no particular similarities to each other and cover needs for which specific community colleges and universities have determined needs.

At the moment, there appears to be only interest by the evolved institutions of higher education in working individually. That being the case, the longevity of the Centers of Excellence may only exist as long as there is interest in the particular topic each is pursuing. On the other hand, the research that each is doing may cause each of them to recognize that working together to some degree could create a synergy that each cannot create on their own.

Since the Centers are literally developing all over the United States, it may be logical that a national organization be formed to bring them together for self-interests and for the possibilities that would help them market themselves as a group. Time will tell.

About the Editor

Darrel W. Staat received his doctorate from the University of Michigan, master's degree from Western Michigan University, and bachelor's degree from Hope College. He has taught a series of eight undergraduate courses and six graduate courses. After retirement, and finding it not to his liking, he assumed the position of coordinator and faculty member in Wingate University's Higher Education Executive Leadership program in January 2015.

Currently he holds the position of coordinator and associate professor of the Higher Education Executive Leadership program. Previously, he held the positions of president of the South Carolina Technical College System in Columbia South Carolina; president of Central Virginia Community College in Lynchburg Virginia; the founding president of York County Community College in Wells Maine, and president of Eastern Maine Community College in Bangor Maine.

His previous publications include:

Leading the Community College: Pathways Through an Exponentially Digital Age (2022)

Virtual Reality in Higher Education: Instruction in an Exponential, Digital Age (2021)

Higher Education Planning in an Exponential Age: A Continuous, Dynamic Process (2021)

Student Focused Learning: Higher Education in an Exponential Digital Era (2020)

A Baseline of Development: Higher Education and Technology (2019)

Exponential Technologies: Higher Education in an Era of Serial Disruptions (2019)

Facing an Exponential Future: Technology and the Community College (2018)

About the Contributors

Roy E. Allen holds a master's degree in criminal justice and an EdS in higher education administration. He is currently the Dean of Public Safety and Human Services at Piedmont Technical College in Roxboro, North Carolina.

Diana Cavender Dymek holds a master's degree in business administration and an Ed.S. in higher education administration. She is currently an adjunct business faculty member at York Technical College in Rock Hill, South Carolina.

Kara McLain Finch holds a master's degree in gerontology and an EdS in higher education administration. She is currently the program head of human services at Stanly Community College in Albemarle, North Carolina.

Candice Geiger holds a master's degree higher education administration and an EdS in higher education administration. She is currently the health care programs director at Midlands Technical College in Columbia, South Carolina.

Cory Glasser holds a master's degree in instructional design and an EdS in higher education administration. He is currently the program coordinator of student financial aid at Central Piedmont Community College in Charlotte, North Carolina.

Shawn Guy holds a master's degree in business and an EdS in higher education administration. He is currently the Director of the TRIO student support services at Alamance Community College in Graham, North Carolina.

Timothy Gwillim holds a master's degree in educational administration, a master's degree in political science, and an EdS in higher education administration. He currently is the dean of workforce training and community engagement at Davidson-Davie Community College in Thomasville, North Carolina.

Lauren Holland holds a master's degree in political science and an EdS in higher education administration. She currently is the associate vice president of corporate and workforce development at Florence Darlington Technical College in Florence, South Carolina.

Amber Lennon-Harmon holds a master's degree in the science in school counseling and an EdS in higher education administration. She is currently the director of career and professional development at Elizabeth City State University in Elizabeth City, North Carolina.

Von Locklear holds a JD degree and an EdS in higher education administration. He is currently a paralegal instructor at Fayetteville Technical and Community College at Fayetteville, North Carolina.

Mark T. Rooze holds a master's degree in English, a master's degree in religion, and an EdS in higher education administration. He is currently the department head of English and Humanities at Florence Darlington Technical College in Florence, South Carolina.

Pamela Shortt holds a master's degree in information systems and operations management and an EdS in higher education administration. She is currently the dean of business and information technology at Forsyth Technical Community College in Winston-Salem, North Carolina.

www.ingramcontent.com/pod-product-compliance
Lightning Source LLC
Chambersburg PA
CBHW032215230426
43672CB00011B/2569